THE ULTIMATE HIGH PROTEIN COTTAGE CHEESE COOKBOOK

Nutritious and Flavorful Cottage Cheese Recipes for Strength, Energy, and Wellness | Full Color Edition

Winona E. Gebo

Manufactured in the United States of America
Interior and Cover Designer: Danielle Rees
Art Producer: Brooke White
Editor: Aaliyah Lyons
Production Editor: Sienna Adams
Production Manager: Sarah Johnson
Photography: Michael Smith

TABLE OF CONTENTS

Introduction 1

Chapter 1: Cottage Cheese Uncovers Hidden Health Secrets............................... 2

The Rich History and Evolution of Cottage Cheese.. 2

Cottage Cheese as a High-Protein Superfood 3

Debunking Myths and Maximizing Benefits... 4

Chapter 2: 4-Week Meal Plan.. 6

Week 1 7

Week 2 8

Week 3 9

Week 4 10

Chapter 3: High-Protein Breakfast... 11

Bacon Cottage Cheese Deviled Eggs 12

Cottage Cheese Almond Pancakes.. 12

Banana Cottage Cheese Oatcakes... 13

Carrot and Oat Cottage Cheese Pancakes 13

Ham And Cottage Cheese Breakfast Quiche 14

Low-Carb Pancakes with Cottage Cheese Topping... 14

TABLE OF CONTENTS

Zucchini Bacon Cottage Cheese Breakfast Casserole...15

Cottage Cheese and Potato Breakfast Bake 15

Pumpkin Cottage Cheese Pancakes..16

Cottage Cheese Berry Breakfast Bowl 16

Chapter 4: Protein-Packed Smoothies and Drinks..**17**

Blueberry-Coconut Pancake Batter Smoothie...18

Golden Milk Shake..18

Strawberry-Banana Cream 19

Green Goddess Smoothie..19

Tropical Cottage Cheese Refresher...20

Chocolate Peanut Butter Power Smoothie 20

Raspberry-Oat Breakfast Smoothie 21

Strawberry-Banana Bliss Smoothie...21

Peachy Vanilla Protein Shake..22

Berry Vanilla Cottage Cheese Blast 22

Mango-Turmeric Immunity Smoothie...23

Berry-Almond Breakfast Shake..23

Chapter 5: Protein-Boosted Salads **24**

Special Chicken Salad 25

Greek Cottage Cheese Salad 25

Perfect Protein Salad with Buttermilk Dressing 26

"Big Mac" Inspired Cottage Cheese Salad 26

Pork Chops and Roasted Winter Squash Salad 27

Creamy Cottage Cheese Shrimp Salad 27

Shredded Chicken and Cabbage Salad 28

Simple Steamed Tomato Cottage Cheese Salad 28

Chicken and Lettuce Salad with Cottage Cheese Dressing 29

Tyrolean Cottage Cheese Egg Salad 29

Chapter 6: Protein-Forward Main Dishes 30

Turkey and Cottage Cheese Bake 31

Cheesy Beef and Cauliflower Skillet 31

Loaded Cottage Cheese Broccoli Baked Potatoes 32

Creamy Cottage Cheese Mac and Cheese 33

Tropical Cottage Cheese Bowl 33

Lentil and Zucchini Pasta Bake 34

Mediterranean Fish and Cottage Cheese Bake 34

TABLE OF CONTENTS

Ground Pork Taco Casserole..35

Filet Mignon with Caramelized Onions..36

Chapter 7: Protein-Enriched Pasta and Pizza 37

Stuffed Pasta Shells with Cottage Cheese...38

Breakfast Pizza with Cottage Cheese...38

Creamy Italian Chicken & Pasta..39

Savory Linguine with Cottage Cheese Pesto..39

Florentine Cottage Cheese Pizza..40

BBQ Chicken & Noodles with Cottage Cheese 40

Chicken & Spinach Skillet..41

Southwest Turkey Lasagna...41

High-Protein Cottage Cheese Pizza...42

Buffalo Chicken Pizza..42

Chapter 8: Protein-Heavy Soups and Stews..43

Halibut Stew..44

Keto Taco Soup..44

Coconut Broccoli Soup..45

Cottage Cheese Zucchini Leek Soup...45

Cottage Cheese Leek Soup 46

Chicken Fajita Soup 46

French Caramelized Onion Soup 47

Roasted Red Pepper Soup 47

Herby Cheese Soup 48

Broccoli Cheese Soup 48

Chapter 9: Protein-Rich Snacks 49

Egg Bites 50

Cauliflower Tots 50

Double Cheese Bites 51

Three-Cheese and Beer Dip 51

Grilled Balsamic Melon and Cheese 52

Spanish Cottage Cheese Bombs 52

Roasted Pepper and Cottage Cheese Dip 53

Parmesan Cottage Cheese Chicken Wings 53

Cottage Cheese and Olive Scones 54

Spicy Sausage and Cottage Cheese Dip 54

Chapter 10: Protein-Enhanced Desserts 55

TABLE OF CONTENTS

Cottage Cheese Strawberry Crepes 56

Peach Cobbler 56

Mango Coconut Cottage Cheese Mousse 57

Poblano and Cheese Frittata...57

Peanut Cheesecake 58

Fluffy Berry Cupcakes...58

Chocolate Protein Crepes..59

Peanut Butter Cheesecake Bites 59

Cherry Mini Cakes...60

Lemon Cheesecake..60

Appendix 1: Measurement Conversion Chart 61

Appendix 2: The Dirty Dozen and Clean Fifteen.........................62

Appendix 3: Index 63

INTRODUCTION

At midlife, I've learned that health isn't about fad diets or expensive supplements—it's about finding simple, honest nutrition. Cottage cheese wasn't something I ever paid much attention to, not until my doctor warned me about losing muscle mass and bone density.

My culinary journey began tentatively. First came the savory experiments: a creamy cottage cheese dip blended with roasted garlic and fresh chives, perfect for afternoon snacking. I discovered it made an incredible base for a quick breakfast parfait, layering it with honey, mixed berries, and a sprinkle of granola. My weekend brunches transformed— cottage cheese pancakes became a family favorite, lighter and more protein-packed than traditional recipes.

The sweet treats surprised me most. I crafted a no-bake cheesecake that was both healthier and more delicious than any I'd made before. Blended smooth with a touch of vanilla and lemon zest, topped with a mixed berry compote, it became my go-to dessert for book club gatherings. Chocolate mousse was another revelation—whipped cottage cheese, cocoa powder, and a drizzle of maple syrup created a decadent yet guilt-free indulgence.

Savory dishes were equally exciting. I developed a killer vegetable lasagna using cottage cheese as a protein-rich replacement for traditional ricotta. Stuffed peppers became a weekly staple, mixing the cheese with quinoa, herbs, and roasted vegetables. Even my salad dressings got an upgrade—a creamy herb dressing that added richness without heavy calories.

My husband would tease me about my newfound obsession. "Honey," he'd say, watching me measure out precise portions, "you're treating that cottage cheese like a scientific experiment." And in a way, I was. After years of yo-yo dieting and complicated meal plans, I'd found something wonderfully straightforward.

The real victory wasn't just nutritional. It was personal. In a phase of life where many women feel invisible, I was taking control—one container of cottage cheese at a time. My kitchen had become a playground of creativity, each recipe a small rebellion against aging's limitations. Who says reinvention stops after midlife? Not me.

DEDICATION

To My Beloved Family, your unwavering support transforms my smallest passions into our shared adventures. My husband, with his gentle teasing and quiet encouragement, has been my greatest ally. Behind every playful joke, I see your genuine love—researching recipes, surprising me with new cooking techniques, standing beside me in the kitchen as we experiment together. You listen, laugh, and love without judgment, turning my quirky cottage cheese obsession into a journey we navigate as a team. Your support isn't just about food; it's about celebrating each other's curiosities and growing together, one delicious moment at a time.

CHAPTER 1: COTTAGE CHEESE UNCOVERS HIDDEN HEALTH SECRETS

THE RICH HISTORY AND EVOLUTION OF COTTAGE CHEESE

Origins and Historical Significance

Cottage cheese isn't just another dairy product—it's a culinary time traveler that has journeyed through centuries of human food culture. Its roots trace back to ancient civilizations where resourceful farmers discovered a brilliant way to preserve milk surplus. The term "cottage cheese" itself tells a story, originating from rural farmhouses and small cottages where women would make cheese in their own kitchens using excess milk from family dairy cows.

Dating back to the Middle Ages in Europe, cottage cheese was a crucial protein source for farming communities. Before refrigeration, transforming milk into a stable, nutrient-dense food was more than a culinary choice—it was a survival strategy. Farmers would collect leftover milk, allow it to naturally sour, and then separate the curds from the whey, creating a protein-rich food that could be stored without spoiling quickly.

How Cottage Cheese Became a Health Food Trend

The transformation of cottage cheese from a humble farm staple to a modern health food is a fascinating journey of nutrition science and cultural shifts. In the mid-20th century, as fitness and dietary awareness began to grow, cottage cheese emerged as a nutritional powerhouse. Bodybuilders and athletes were among the first to recognize its exceptional protein content and low-calorie profile.

The 1950s and 1960s saw cottage cheese become a staple of diet culture. Weight loss programs and nutrition guides frequently recommended it as a "diet food" due to its high protein and low-fat content. Hollywood celebrities and fitness icons of the era often showcased cottage cheese in their dietary regimens, further popularizing its image as a health-conscious food choice.

By the 1970s and 1980s, cottage cheese had transcended its initial diet food reputation. Nutritionists began highlighting its comprehensive nutritional profile—rich in calcium, phosphorus, and B vitamins. It wasn't just about weight loss anymore; it was recognized as a genuinely nutritious food that could support muscle development, bone health, and overall wellness.

Traditional Methods of Making Cottage Cheese

Traditional cottage cheese production is an art form that combines simple ingredients with precise techniques. The process begins with fresh milk—traditionally from cows, though goat and sheep milk variations exist. Farmers would start by introducing a bacterial culture to the milk, allowing it to acidify and develop flavor.

The acidification process causes milk proteins to coagulate, forming soft curds. Skilled cheesemakers would then carefully cut these curds, allowing whey to separate. The curds are gently heated and stirred, which helps determine the cheese's final texture. The size of the curd cut and the heating duration directly influence the cottage cheese's consistency—smaller cuts create firmer cheese, while larger cuts result in a softer, creamier texture.

After separation, the curds are washed with cool water to stop the acidification process and remove excess whey. This washing also helps achieve the characteristic mild flavor of cottage cheese. The final step involves adding a light cream or milk dressing, giving cottage cheese its signature creamy appearance.

Modern industrial production has streamlined these traditional methods, but artisanal cheesemakers still honor the original techniques. Small-batch producers continue to create cottage cheese using methods passed down through generations, maintaining the food's rich cultural heritage.

From ancient farmhouse kitchens to modern health food stores, cottage cheese has continuously reinvented itself. It remains a testament to human ingenuity—a simple food that has adapted, survived, and thrived through changing dietary landscapes.

COTTAGE CHEESE AS A HIGH-PROTEIN SUPERFOOD

WHY COTTAGE CHEESE IS A PROTEIN POWERHOUSE

Imagine a food that's like a secret weapon for nutrition - that's cottage cheese in a nutshell. Unlike many protein sources that are either bland or complicated to prepare, cottage cheese offers a unique combination of convenience, taste, and nutritional punch. What makes it stand out is its impressive protein content, particularly casein protein, which is a slow-digesting protein that provides a steady release of amino acids to your body.

A single serving of cottage cheese packs a serious protein punch, typically offering around 14 to 25 grams of protein per cup, depending on the fat content. This is remarkable compared to many other protein sources. What's even more interesting is the protein quality - it contains all nine essential amino acids that our bodies can't produce on their own. These amino acids are crucial for muscle repair, immune function, and overall body maintenance.

THE SCIENCE BEHIND PROTEIN AND MUSCLE GROWTH

Protein isn't just about bulking up - it's about cellular repair, metabolic function, and overall body health. When you consume protein, your body breaks it down into amino acids, which act like building blocks for muscle tissue. Cottage cheese's specific protein composition makes it particularly effective for muscle maintenance and growth.

Casein protein, the primary protein in cottage cheese, has a unique characteristic: it digests slowly. This slow digestion means a sustained release of amino acids into your bloodstream. For athletes and fitness enthusiasts, this translates to prolonged muscle protein synthesis. Think of it like a slow-burning fuel that keeps your muscles nourished over an extended period, especially beneficial during sleep or between meals.

Scientific research has shown that consuming slow-digesting proteins like casein before bed can significantly improve muscle recovery and growth. This makes cottage cheese an ideal late-night snack for those looking to support their fitness goals. The protein helps prevent muscle breakdown and provides essential nutrients for overnight recovery.

COTTAGE CHEESE VS. OTHER PROTEIN SOURCES

Let's break down how cottage cheese compares to other protein sources. Unlike protein powders that can be processed and artificial, cottage cheese is a whole food with additional nutritional benefits. Compared to chicken or eggs, it offers similar protein content but with a different nutritional profile.

Greek yogurt is often considered a protein-rich food, but cottage cheese typically contains more protein per serving. While Greek yogurt averages around 15-20 grams of protein per cup, cottage cheese can offer up to 25 grams. Plus, cottage cheese tends to be lower in sugar and offers more versatility in cooking and preparation.

Plant-based protein sources like tofu or legumes often require more complex preparation and may lack some essential amino acids. Cottage cheese provides a complete protein source that's ready to eat, requiring minimal preparation. For vegetarians who consume dairy, it's an excellent protein alternative that doesn't rely on processed meat substitutes.

The nutritional benefits extend beyond protein. Cottage cheese is rich in calcium, phosphorus, and B vitamins. It supports bone health, helps regulate metabolism, and provides essential nutrients that many other protein sources might lack.

What truly sets cottage cheese apart is its adaptability. It can be a savory breakfast, a post-workout snack, a cooking ingredient, or even a dessert base. From protein pancakes to creamy dips, from salad toppings to smoothie enhancers, cottage cheese proves that healthy eating doesn't have to be boring or complicated.

DEBUNKING MYTHS AND MAXIMIZING BENEFITS

✓ **COMMON MISCONCEPTIONS ABOUT COTTAGE CHEESE**

Let's address the elephant in the room - cottage cheese has suffered from some seriously unfair reputation issues. Many people imagine it as a bland, diet-food relic from the 1980s, something only health-obsessed individuals would touch. The truth? It's a versatile, delicious food that's been misunderstood for far too long.

One prevalent myth is that cottage cheese is only for people trying to lose weight. While it's true that cottage cheese can be an excellent component of a weight management plan, its benefits extend far beyond calorie counting. Another misconception is that all cottage cheese tastes the same - bland and rubbery. Modern cottage cheese varieties come in different fat contents, textures, and flavors, from creamy to chunky, mild to tangy.

Some folks believe cottage cheese is difficult to digest or only suitable for certain age groups. In reality, it's a nutrient-dense food that can benefit everyone from children to seniors. The protein and calcium content make it an excellent choice for growing bodies and aging bones alike.

✓ **THE ROLE OF COTTAGE CHEESE IN VARIOUS DIETS**

Cottage cheese has become a chameleon in the dietary world, fitting seamlessly into multiple eating approaches. For athletes and bodybuilders, it's a protein-packed recovery food. Its slow-releasing protein helps muscle repair and provides sustained energy. Keto dieters appreciate its high protein and low-carb profile, using it as a versatile ingredient in both savory and sweet preparations.

Vegetarian diets often struggle with protein sources, and cottage cheese emerges as a hero. It provides complete proteins without relying on meat, making it an excellent nutritional supplement for those avoiding animal flesh. For those following Mediterranean or balanced dietary approaches, cottage cheese fits perfectly as a protein-rich, calcium-dense food.

Interestingly, cottage cheese has found its way into increasingly diverse dietary plans. Intermittent fasters use it as a satisfying, nutrient-dense food during eating windows. People managing blood sugar levels appreciate its low glycemic index and ability to provide steady energy.

✓ **BEST WAYS TO INCORPORATE COTTAGE CHEESE INTO DAILY MEALS**

Forget the notion that cottage cheese is just a boring diet food. Modern culinary creativity has transformed it into a versatile ingredient that can elevate multiple dishes. Breakfast becomes exciting with cottage cheese pancakes, smoothie additions, or as a creamy toast topping. Mix it with fresh herbs for a savory spread, or blend it with fruits for a quick, protein-rich morning meal.

Lunch and dinner options are equally exciting. Use cottage cheese as a protein-packed salad topping, a creamy pasta sauce base, or a filling for stuffed vegetables. It can replace ricotta in lasagnas, add creaminess to scrambled eggs, or serve as a base for quick dips and spreads.

Dessert lovers aren't left out. Blend cottage cheese with cocoa for a protein-rich chocolate mousse, use it in cheesecake recipes, or mix it with fruits for a creamy, guilt-free dessert. Bakers can even use it as a partial butter or oil replacement in certain recipes, adding moisture and protein.

The key is experimentation. Start with small quantities, mix with flavors you enjoy, and gradually explore its versatility. Whether you're a fitness enthusiast, a busy professional, or someone simply looking to add more nutrition to your diet, cottage cheese offers something for everyone.

Ultimately, cottage cheese is more than just a food - it's a nutritional ally waiting to be discovered and enjoyed in countless delicious ways.

CHAPTER 2: 4-WEEK MEAL PLAN

WEEK 1

Day 1:

Breakfast: **Cottage Cheese Almond Pancakes**

Lunch: **Turkey and Cottage Cheese Bake**

Snack: **Double Cheese Bites**

Dinner: **Tyrolean Cottage Cheese Egg Salad**

Total for the day:

Calories: **1702**; Fat: **128g**; Carbs: **34.4g**; Fiber: **8.8g**; Protein: **111.6g**

Day 2:

Breakfast: **Ham And Cottage Cheese Breakfast Quiche**

Lunch: **Turkey and Cottage Cheese Bake**

Snack: **Double Cheese Bites (2 Serves)**

Dinner: **Tropical Cottage Cheese Bowl**

Total for the day:

Calories: **1952**; Fat: **132g**; Protein: **143.2g**; Carbs: **55.8g**; Fiber: **8.6g**

Day 3:

Breakfast: **Cottage Cheese Almond Pancakes**

Lunch: **Tyrolean Cottage Cheese Egg Salad**

Snack: **Roasted Pepper and Cottage Cheese Dip (2 Serves)**

Dinner: **Perfect Protein Salad with Buttermilk Dressing**

Total for the day:

Calories: **1857**; Fat: **124g**; Carbs: **49g**; Fiber: **16g**; Protein: **93g**

Day 4:

Breakfast: **Ham And Cottage Cheese Breakfast Quiche**

Lunch: **Tropical Cottage Cheese Bowl**

Snack: **Roasted Pepper and Cottage Cheese Dip (2 Serves)**

Dinner: **Turkey and Cottage Cheese Bake**

Total for the day:

Calories: **2066**; Fat: **141g**; Protein: **113g**; Carbs: **32g**; Fiber: **6g**

Day 5:

Breakfast: **Cottage Cheese Almond Pancakes**

Lunch: **Filet Mignon with Caramelized Onions**

Snack: **Double Cheese Bites (2 Serves)**

Dinner: **Tyrolean Cottage Cheese Egg Salad**

Total for the day:

Calories: **2031**; Fat: **156g**; Carbs: **53.8g**; Fiber: **11.6g**; Protein: **134.2g**

Day 6:

Breakfast: **Ham And Cottage Cheese Breakfast Quiche**

Lunch: **Filet Mignon with Caramelized Onions**

Snack: **Double Cheese Bites**

Dinner: **Turkey and Cottage Cheese Bake**

Total for the day:

Calories: **1811**; Fat: **136g**; Protein: **135.6g**; Carbs: **37.4g**; Fiber: **5.8g**

Day 7:

Breakfast: **Cottage Cheese Almond Pancakes**

Lunch: **Tyrolean Cottage Cheese Egg Salad**

Snack: **Roasted Pepper and Cottage Cheese Dip (2 Serves)**

Dinner: **Filet Mignon with Caramelized Onions**

Total for the day:

Calories: **2019**; Fat: **142g**; Carbs: **47g**; Fiber: **10g**; Protein: **109g**

WEEK 2

Day 1:

Breakfast: **Cottage Cheese Berry Breakfast Bowl**

Lunch: **Cheesy Beef and Cauliflower Skillet**

Snack: **Three-Cheese and Beer Dip (2 Serves)**

Dinner: **BBQ Chicken & Noodles with Cottage Cheese**

Total for the day:

Calories: 1850; Fat: 100g; Protein: 131g; Carbs: 71g; Fiber: 10g

Day 2:

Breakfast: **Low-Carb Pancakes with Cottage Cheese Topping**

Lunch: **Cheesy Beef and Cauliflower Skillet**

Snack: **Three-Cheese and Beer Dip**

Dinner: **Lentil and Zucchini Pasta Bake**

Total for the day:

Calories: 1749; Fat: 113g; Carbs: 88g; Protein: 94g; Fiber: 18g

Day 3:

Breakfast: **Cottage Cheese Berry Breakfast Bowl**

Lunch: **Lentil and Zucchini Pasta Bake**

Snack: **Cottage Cheese and Olive Scones**

Dinner: **Cheesy Beef and Cauliflower Skillet**

Total for the day:

Calories: 1865; Fat: 102g; Protein: 112g; Carbs: 121g; Fiber: 27g

Day 4:

Breakfast: **Low-Carb Pancakes with Cottage Cheese Topping**

Lunch: **Chicken & Spinach Skillet**

Snack: **Cottage Cheese and Olive Scones**

Dinner: **Cheesy Beef and Cauliflower Skillet**

Total for the day:

Calories: 1898; Fat: 137g; Protein: 115g; Carbs: 54g; Fiber: 17g

Day 5:

Breakfast: **Cottage Cheese Berry Breakfast Bowl**

Lunch: **BBQ Chicken & Noodles with Cottage Cheese**

Snack: **Three-Cheese and Beer Dip (2 Serves)**

Dinner: **Lentil and Zucchini Pasta Bake**

Total for the day:

Calories: 1823; Fat: 77g; Protein: 121g; Carbs: 117g; Fiber: 18g

Day 6:

Breakfast: **Low-Carb Pancakes with Cottage Cheese Topping**

Lunch: **BBQ Chicken & Noodles with Cottage Cheese**

Snack: **Three-Cheese and Beer Dip**

Dinner: **Chicken & Spinach Skillet**

Total for the day:

Calories: 1856; Fat: 112g; Protein: 124g; Carbs: 50g; Fiber: 8g

Day 7:

Breakfast: **Low-Carb Pancakes with Cottage Cheese Topping**

Lunch: **Chicken & Spinach Skillet**

Snack: **Cottage Cheese and Olive Scones**

Dinner: **BBQ Chicken & Noodles with Cottage Cheese**

Total for the day:

Calories: 1806; Fat: 112g; Protein: 114g; Carbs: 58g; Fiber: 16g

WEEK 3

Day 1:

Breakfast: Banana Cottage Cheese Oatcakes

Lunch: Loaded Cottage Cheese Broccoli Baked Potatoes

Snack: Spanish Cottage Cheese Bombs (2 Serves)

Dinner: Mediterranean Fish and Cottage Cheese Bake

Total for the day:

Calories: 2006; Fat: 120g; Carbs: 125g; Protein: 127g; Fiber: 21g

Day 2:

Breakfast: Zucchini Bacon Cottage Cheese Breakfast Casserole

Lunch: High-Protein Cottage Cheese Pizza

Snack: Spanish Cottage Cheese Bombs (2 Serves)

Dinner: Loaded Cottage Cheese Broccoli Baked Potatoes

Total for the day:

Calories: 1929; Fat: 135.3g; Carbs: 99.3g; Protein: 98.7g; Fiber: 13g

Day 3:

Breakfast: Banana Cottage Cheese Oatcakes

Lunch: High-Protein Cottage Cheese Pizza

Snack: Spanish Cottage Cheese Bombs (2 Serves)

Dinner: Chicken and Lettuce Salad with Cottage Cheese Dressing

Total for the day:

Calories: 1971; Fat: 110g; Carbs: 99g; Protein: 100g; Fiber: 13g

Day 4:

Breakfast: Chocolate Peanut Butter Power Smoothie

Lunch: Mediterranean Fish and Cottage Cheese Bake

Snack: Spicy Sausage and Cottage Cheese Dip (2 Serves)

Dinner: High-Protein Cottage Cheese Pizza

Total for the day:

Calories: 1814; Fat: 94.4g; Protein: 93.2g; Carbs: 89.8g; Fiber: 15.2g

Day 5:

Breakfast: Zucchini Bacon Cottage Cheese Breakfast Casserole

Lunch: Mediterranean Fish and Cottage Cheese Bake

Snack: Spanish Cottage Cheese Bombs (2 Serves)

Dinner: High-Protein Cottage Cheese Pizza

Total for the day:

Calories: 1896; Fat: 124.3g; Protein: 106.7g; Carbs: 71.3g; Fiber: 10g

Day 6:

Breakfast: Golden Milk Shake

Lunch: Mediterranean Fish and Cottage Cheese Bake

Snack: Spicy Sausage and Cottage Cheese Dip (2 Serves)

Dinner: High-Protein Cottage Cheese Pizza

Total for the day:

Calories: 1784; Protein: 100.2g; Carbs: 63.8g; Fat: 94.4g; Fiber: 10.2g

Day 7:

Breakfast: Zucchini Bacon Cottage Cheese Breakfast Casserole

Lunch: Chicken and Lettuce Salad with Cottage Cheese Dressing

Snack: Spicy Sausage and Cottage Cheese Dip (2 Serves)

Dinner: High-Protein Cottage Cheese Pizza

Total for the day:

Calories: 1804; Fat: 103.7g; Protein: 84.9g; Carbs: 45.1g; Fiber: 5.2g

WEEK 4

Day 1:

Breakfast: **Pumpkin Cottage Cheese Pancakes**

Lunch: **Special Chicken Salad**

Snack: **Parmesan Cottage Cheese Chicken Wings (2 Serves)**

Dinner: **Ground Pork Taco Casserole**

Total for the day:

Calories: **2001**; Carbs: **58.8g**; Protein: **116.1g**; Fat: **124.1g**; Fiber: **6.9g**

Day 2:

Breakfast: **Raspberry-Oat Breakfast Smoothie**

Lunch: **Ground Pork Taco Casserole**

Snack: **Parmesan Cottage Cheese Chicken Wings (2 Serves)**

Dinner: **Special Chicken Salad**

Total for the day:

Calories: **2026**; Fat: **125.1g**; Protein: **116.1g**; Carbs: **65.6g**; Fiber: **11.9g**

Day 3:

Breakfast: **Pumpkin Cottage Cheese Pancakes**

Lunch: **Buffalo Chicken Pizza**

Snack: **Grilled Balsamic Melon and Cheese (2 Serves)**

Dinner: **Ground Pork Taco Casserole**

Total for the day:

Calories: **1785**; Carbs: **118.2g**; Protein: **96g**; Fat: **89g**; Fiber: **11g**

Day 4:

Breakfast: **Berry Vanilla Cottage Cheese Blast**

Lunch: **Special Chicken Salad**

Snack: **Parmesan Cottage Cheese Chicken Wings (2 Serves)**

Dinner: **Buffalo Chicken Pizza**

Total for the day:

Calories: **1968**; Fat: **103.1g**; Protein: **109.6g**; Carbs: **69.6g**; Fiber: **11.2g**

Day 5:

Breakfast: **Pumpkin Cottage Cheese Pancakes**

Lunch: **Buffalo Chicken Pizza**

Snack: **Grilled Balsamic Melon and Cheese (2 Serves)**

Dinner: **Ground Pork Taco Casserole**

Total for the day:

Calories: **1785**; Carbs: **118.2g**; Protein: **96g**; Fat: **89g**; Fiber: **11g**

Day 6:

Breakfast: **Bacon Cottage Cheese Deviled Eggs**

Lunch: **Greek Cottage Cheese Salad**

Snack: **Parmesan Cottage Cheese Chicken Wings**

Dinner: **Special Chicken Salad**

Total for the day:

Calories: **1767**; Fat: **116.4g**; Carbs: **40.4g**; Protein: **94.7g**; Fiber: **12.7g**

Day 7:

Breakfast: **Bacon Cottage Cheese Deviled Eggs**

Lunch: **Greek Cottage Cheese Salad**

Snack: **Parmesan Cottage Cheese Chicken Wings**

Dinner: **Buffalo Chicken Pizza**

Total for the day:

Calories: **1737**; Fat: **87.3g**; Carbs: **61.8g**; Protein: **94.6g**; Fiber: **12.8g**

CHAPTER 3: HIGH-PROTEIN BREAKFAST

BACON COTTAGE CHEESE DEVILED EGGS

Prep time: 5 minutes | Cook time: 15 minutes |Serves 4

- 4 ounces bacon, diced
- 10 large eggs
- 1/3 cup cottage cheese
- 1 tablespoon Dijon mustard
- 1 roasted red bell pepper, chopped
- Kosher salt and freshly ground black pepper, to taste
- 1 tablespoon fresh cilantro, minced, plus extra for garnish

1. Preheat a skillet over medium-high heat. Add bacon and fry until crisp; set aside.

2. Place eggs in a medium saucepan. Add water to cover the eggs by 1 inch and bring to a full boil.
3. Turn off heat, cover the pan, and let sit for 9 to 10 minutes.
4. Transfer eggs to an ice bath. When cool enough to handle, peel away the shells; rinse eggs under cold running water. Cut eggs in half lengthwise and separate the whites from the yolks.
5. In a medium bowl, combine the egg yolks with the reserved bacon, cottage cheese, mustard, bell pepper, salt, and black pepper. Mix until smooth and creamy.

6. Spoon or pipe the filling into the egg white halves, arrange on a serving platter, and garnish with fresh cilantro. Enjoy!

Per Serving

Calories: **393**| Fat: **22.3g** | Carbs: **4.8g** | Protein: **18.6g** | Fiber: **0.8g**

COTTAGE CHEESE ALMOND PANCAKES

Prep time: 10 minutes | Cook time: 20 minutes | Serves 4

- 2 cups low-fat cottage cheese
- 4 egg whites
- 2 whole eggs
- 1 tablespoon pure vanilla extract
- 1½ cups almond flour
- Nonstick cooking spray
- Fresh berries or sliced fruit for serving (optional)

1. In a blender, combine cottage cheese, egg whites, whole eggs, and vanilla. Pulse until well combined.
2. Add the almond flour to the blender and blend until the

batter is completely smooth.
3. Heat a large nonstick skillet over medium heat and lightly coat with cooking spray.
4. For each pancake, pour ¼ cup of batter into the skillet, cooking 4 pancakes at a time. Cook until the bottoms are firm and golden brown, about 4 minutes.
5. Flip pancakes and cook the other side until golden and cooked through, about 3 minutes.
6. Transfer pancakes to a warm plate and repeat with remaining batter.
7. Serve warm with fresh fruit of your choice.

Per Serving

Calories: **344** |Fat: **22g** | Carbs: **11g** | Fiber: **4g** | Protein: **29g**

BANANA COTTAGE CHEESE OATCAKES

Prep time: 5 minutes | Cook time: 10 minutes | Serves 2

- 1 cup old-fashioned rolled oats
- 6 egg whites (or 1 cup plus 2 tablespoons liquid egg white substitute)
- 1 ripe banana, peeled and sliced
- 1 cup 2% cottage cheese
- ½ teaspoon ground cinnamon
- 1 tablespoon granulated sugar
- Cooking spray

1. In a medium bowl, combine oats, egg whites, banana, cottage cheese, cinnamon, and sugar. Mix with a spatula until the batter is smooth. You can also pulse in a blender for a smoother consistency.
2. Coat a medium non-stick skillet with cooking spray and heat over medium heat.
3. Pour about one-quarter of the batter (approximately ½ cup) into the hot pan. Cook until golden brown on the bottom, about 1 to 2 minutes.
4. Flip the oatcake with a spatula and cook another 30 to 60 seconds, until golden brown and firm. Transfer to a plate.
5. Reapply cooking spray and repeat with remaining batter to make a total of 4

oatcakes.
6. Serve warm, topped with additional sliced bananas, a dollop of cottage cheese, or a drizzle of honey if desired.

Per Serving

Calories: **375** | Fat: **7g** | Carbs: **45g** | Protein: **23g** | Fiber: **6g**

CARROT AND OAT COTTAGE CHEESE PANCAKES

Prep time: 10 minutes | Cook time: 8 minutes | Serves 4

- ¼ cup plain Greek yogurt
- 1 tablespoon pure maple syrup, plus more for serving if desired
- 1 cup rolled oats
- 1 cup low-fat cottage cheese
- 1 cup carrots, finely shredded
- ½ cup unsweetened plain almond milk
- 2 large eggs
- 1 teaspoon baking powder
- 2 tablespoons ground flaxseed
- ½ teaspoon ground cinnamon
- 2 teaspoons vegetable oil, divided

1. In a small bowl, stir together the Greek yogurt and maple syrup. Set aside.
2. Add the rolled oats to a blender and pulse until ground into a flour-like consistency.
3. Add the cottage cheese, shredded carrots, almond milk, eggs, baking powder, flaxseed, and cinnamon to the blender. Process until fully mixed and smooth.
4. Heat 1 teaspoon of vegetable oil in a large skillet over medium heat.
5. Pour ¼ cup of batter into the skillet for each pancake. Cook for 1 to 2 minutes until bubbles form on the surface.
6. Gently flip each pancake with a spatula and cook for

1 to 2 minutes more, until golden brown around the edges.
7. Repeat with the remaining oil and batter.
8. Serve warm, topped with the maple yogurt mixture.

Per Serving

Calories: **227** | Fat: **8.1g** | Protein: **14.9g** | Carbs: **24.2g** | Fiber: **4.0g**

HAM AND COTTAGE CHEESE BREAKFAST QUICHE

Prep time: 10 minutes | Cook time: 45 minutes | Serves 4

- Nonstick cooking spray
- 4 large eggs
- 1½ cups egg whites
- 1 cup reduced-fat cottage cheese (1%)
- 5 bacon slices, cooked and crumbled
- ½ cup extra-lean ham, finely chopped
- ¼ cup feta cheese, crumbled
- ½ onion, finely chopped
- 1 green bell pepper, finely chopped
- ½ teaspoon sea salt
- ¼ teaspoon freshly ground black pepper

1. Preheat the oven to 350°F. Coat the bottom and sides of an 8-by-8-inch square glass baking dish with nonstick cooking spray.
2. In a large bowl, combine the eggs, egg whites, cottage cheese, bacon, ham, feta, onion, bell pepper, salt, and pepper. Whisk until well mixed.
3. Pour the mixture into the prepared baking dish, spreading evenly.
4. Bake for 45 minutes, or until the center is set and a knife inserted in the center comes out clean.
5. Remove from the oven and let cool for 5-10 minutes before cutting.

6. Cut into 8 equal pieces. Serve 2 pieces per person, or store in airtight containers for meal prep.

Per Serving

Calories: **322** | Fat: **18g** | Protein: **33g** | Carbs: **6g** | Fiber: **1g**

LOW-CARB PANCAKES WITH COTTAGE CHEESE TOPPING

Prep time: 10 minutes | Cook time: 1 hour 15 minutes | Serves 4

For the Pancakes:
- 2 tablespoons coconut oil
- 4 large eggs
- 8 ounces cream cheese, softened
- ¼ teaspoon kosher salt
- 1 teaspoon granulated sugar substitute
- 1 teaspoon ground psyllium husk powder

For the Cottage Cheese Topping:
- 6 ounces cottage cheese, at room temperature
- 4 tablespoons low-carb mayonnaise, preferably homemade
- 1 small shallot, minced
- Sea salt and freshly ground black pepper, to taste

1. In a medium bowl, thoroughly combine all the pancake ingredients until smooth.
2. Spray the inner pot of your Instant Pot with nonstick cooking spray.
3. Pour half of the pancake mixture into the pot.
4. Secure the lid and set the pressure valve to sealing position.
5. Select "Multigrain" mode and set to Low pressure for 35 minutes.
6. When cooking is complete, allow for a natural pressure release (about 10-15 minutes).
7. Carefully remove the lid and transfer the pancake to a serving plate.
8. Repeat steps 2-7 with the remaining pancake mixture.
9. While the second pancake

is cooking, prepare the topping: In a small bowl, combine cottage cheese, mayonnaise, minced shallot, salt, and pepper. Mix until well blended.

10. To serve, spread the cottage cheese topping over the warm pancakes and enjoy.

Per Serving

Calories: **450** | Fat: **40g** | Carbs: **8g** | Protein: **18g** | Fiber: **2g**

ZUCCHINI BACON COTTAGE CHEESE BREAKFAST CASSEROLE

Prep time: **10 minutes** | Cook time: **25 minutes** | Serves **6**

- ½ pound zucchini, grated and squeezed dry
- 1 white onion, chopped
- 1 clove garlic, minced
- 6 slices bacon, chopped
- 1 cup Colby cheese, shredded
- 1 cup cottage cheese, at room temperature
- 8 large eggs, beaten
- ½ cup Greek yogurt, at room temperature
- Sea salt and freshly ground black pepper, to taste
- ¼ teaspoon dried marjoram
- ¼ teaspoon dried rosemary
- 1 teaspoon dried parsley flakes

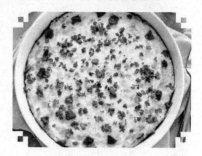

1. Add 1 cup of water and place a metal trivet in the bottom of your Instant Pot.
2. In a large bowl, combine all ingredients and mix until well incorporated.
3. Lightly grease a casserole dish that fits inside your Instant Pot, then spoon the mixture into it.
4. Carefully lower the casserole dish onto the trivet in the Instant Pot.
5. Secure the lid and ensure the pressure valve is set to sealing position.
6. Select "Manual" (or "Pressure Cook") mode on High pressure and set for 20 minutes.
7. Once cooking is complete, perform a quick pressure release by carefully turning the valve to venting.
8. When the pressure has fully released, carefully remove the lid and lift out the casserole dish.
9. Let stand for 5 minutes before serving.

Per Serving

Calories: **320** | Fat: **24.3g** | Carbs: **5.3g** | Protein: **19.7g** | Sugars: **2.9g**

COTTAGE CHEESE AND POTATO BREAKFAST BAKE

Prep time: **20 minutes** | Cook time: **1 hour** | Serves **8**

- 4 cups frozen diced hash brown potatoes, thawed
- ½ cup frozen whole-kernel corn, thawed
- ¼ cup roasted red bell peppers, chopped
- 1½ cups reduced-fat Colby-Monterey Jack cheese, shredded and divided
- 10 large eggs (or 2½ cups liquid egg substitute)
- ½ cup fat-free cottage cheese
- ½ teaspoon dried oregano
- ¼ teaspoon garlic powder
- 4 medium green onions, chopped (about ¼ cup)
- Cooking spray

1. Heat oven to 350°F. Spray an 11x7-inch (2-quart) glass baking dish with cooking spray.
2. In the baking dish, layer the potatoes, corn, bell peppers, and 1 cup of the shredded cheese.
3. In a medium bowl, whisk together eggs, cottage cheese, oregano, and garlic powder until well blended.
4. Slowly pour the egg mixture over the potato mixture in the baking dish.
5. Sprinkle with green onions and the remaining ½ cup shredded cheese.
6. Cover with aluminum foil and bake for 30 minutes.
7. Uncover and bake about 30 minutes longer or until a knife inserted in the center comes out clean.
8. Let stand for 5 to 10 minutes before cutting and serving.

Per Serving

Calories: **240** | Fat: **11g** | Carbs: **18g** | Fiber: **2g** | Protein: **16g**

PUMPKIN COTTAGE CHEESE PANCAKES

Prep time: 20 minutes | Cook time: 10 minutes | Serves 3

- 1½ cups rolled oats
- ½ cup pumpkin puree
- ½ cup cottage cheese
- 2 large eggs
- 2 tablespoons pure maple syrup
- 2 teaspoons baking powder
- 1 teaspoon pumpkin pie spice
- ¼ teaspoon salt
- Butter or cooking spray for greasing

1. Add all ingredients to a high-powered blender and blend until smooth. Let the batter rest while you preheat the pan.
2. Heat a large non-stick skillet or griddle over medium heat. Lightly coat with butter or cooking spray.
3. When the pan is hot, pour about ¼ cup of batter for each pancake.
4. Use the back of a spoon to gently spread the batter into a circular shape if needed.
5. Cook for 2-4 minutes, or until bubbles form around the edges and the pancakes begin to puff up slightly.
6. Flip and cook for another 1-2 minutes on the other side, until golden brown.
7. Serve warm with additional maple syrup, a dollop of cottage cheese, or fresh fruit if desired.

Per Serving

Calories: **295** | Carbs: **41.2** | Protein: **16g** | Fat: **7g** | Fiber: **3g**

COTTAGE CHEESE BERRY BREAKFAST BOWL

Prep time: 5 minutes | Cook time: 10 minutes | Serves 3

- 2 cups reduced-fat cottage cheese (2%)
- 1 cup nonfat vanilla Greek yogurt
- 1 cup fresh blueberries or raspberries
- 3 tablespoons low-sugar blueberry or mixed berry jam
- 3 tablespoons protein nut butter or regular nut butter (peanut, almond, etc.)
- 3 tablespoons toasted pecan pieces or sliced almonds (optional)

1. For each serving, combine in a bowl or storage container:
    - cup cottage cheese
    - 1/3 cup Greek yogurt
    - 1/3 cup fresh berries
    - 1 tablespoon low-sugar jam
    - 1 tablespoon nut butter
    - 1 tablespoon toasted nuts (if using)
2. Stir well to combine all ingredients.
3. Enjoy immediately or seal in airtight containers for meal prep. These breakfast bowls will keep in the refrigerator for up to 3 days.

Per Serving

Calories: **336** | Fat: **9g** | Protein: **30g** | Carbs: **27g** | Fiber: **3g**

CHAPTER 4: PROTEIN-PACKED SMOOTHIES AND DRINKS

BLUEBERRY-COCONUT PANCAKE BATTER SMOOTHIE

Prep time: **5 minutes** | Cook time: **none** | Serves **1**

- ½ cup coconut water
- 1 cup low-fat buttermilk
- ¼ cup 2% milkfat cottage cheese
- ¼ cup 2% Greek yogurt
- 1 tablespoon coconut flour
- 2 tablespoons honey or date paste
- 1 tablespoon unsweetened shredded coconut
- ½ teaspoon baking soda
- ¼ cup fresh blueberries, plus more for garnish

1. In a high-speed blender, combine the coconut water, buttermilk, cottage cheese, yogurt, coconut flour, honey, shredded coconut, and baking soda. Blend on medium-high speed until completely smooth, about 30-45 seconds.
2. Add the fresh blueberries and pulse 3-4 times just until slightly broken up but still visible throughout the mixture.
3. Pour the pancake smoothie into a tall glass and garnish with a small handful of fresh blueberries on top. Serve immediately with a straw and spoon.
4. Chef's Tip: For an extra protein boost, add a scoop of vanilla protein powder. If you prefer a thicker smoothie, reduce the

coconut water to ¼ cup or add 2-3 ice cubes before blending.

Per Serving

Calories: **431** | Protein: **24g** | Carbs: **67g** | Fat: **9g** | Fiber: **3g**

GOLDEN MILK SHAKE

Prep time: **10 minutes** | Cook time: **none** | Serves **1**

- 1 cup unsweetened vanilla coconut milk
- ¼ cup vanilla whey protein powder
- ½ cup 2% low-sodium cottage cheese
- ½ tablespoon coconut oil
- 1 teaspoon ground ginger
- ½ teaspoon ground turmeric
- ½ teaspoon ground cinnamon
- ¼ teaspoon ground black pepper
- 2 teaspoons powdered stevia (or to taste)
- ½ cup crushed ice

1. Combine the coconut milk, protein powder, cottage cheese, coconut oil, ginger, turmeric, cinnamon, black pepper, stevia, and ice in a blender. Blend on low for 30 seconds, or until the ingredients are well incorporated.
2. Scrape the sides of the blender with a rubber spatula. Blend on high for one additional minute, or until the shake is smooth and creamy.
3. Transfer to a glass and serve immediately.
4. Chef's Tip: The black pepper helps your body absorb the anti-inflammatory benefits of turmeric. For extra

warmth and spice, add a pinch of cayenne pepper or a small piece of fresh ginger root instead of the ground ginger.

Per Serving

Calories: **320** | Protein: **25g** | Carbs: **12g** | Fat: **18g** | Fiber: **2g**

STRAWBERRY-BANANA CREAM

Prep time: **5 minutes** | Cook time: **none** | Serves **1**

- 1 cup frozen strawberries
- 1 ripe medium banana
- ½ cup 2% milkfat cottage cheese
- ½ cup unsweetened almond milk
- 1 tablespoon honey (or pure maple syrup)
- ½ teaspoon pure vanilla extract

1. Add frozen strawberries, banana, cottage cheese, almond milk, honey, and vanilla extract to a blender.
2. Blend on high speed until smooth and creamy, about 1-2 minutes. If the mixture is too thick, add a splash more almond milk.
3. Pour into a tall glass and serve immediately.
4. Chef's Tip: For an extra-cold treat, freeze the peeled banana chunks the night before. To add more protein, include a scoop of your favorite unflavored or vanilla protein powder.

Per Serving

Calories: **280** | Fat: **7.0g** | Protein: **15.0g** | Carbs: **45.0g** | Fiber: **6.0g**

GREEN GODDESS SMOOTHIE

Prep time: **5 minutes** | Cook time: **none** | Serves **1**

- 1 cup fresh spinach, packed
- ½ medium cucumber, peeled and chopped (about 1 cup)
- ½ green apple, cored and chopped
- ¼ cup 2% milkfat cottage cheese
- ½ cup water or coconut water
- 1 tablespoon fresh lemon juice
- 1 teaspoon fresh ginger, grated
- 3-4 ice cubes (optional)

1. Add spinach, cucumber, green apple, cottage cheese, water, lemon juice, ginger, and ice (if using) to a high-speed blender.
2. Blend on high until very smooth, about 60-90 seconds, stopping to scrape down the sides if necessary.
3. Pour into a glass and enjoy immediately.
4. Chef's Tip: For a sweeter smoothie, add a teaspoon of honey or a pitted date. You can also substitute kale for spinach, though the flavor will be more robust.

Per Serving

Calories: **150** | Fat: **3.0g** | Protein: **10.0g** | Carbs: **22.0g** | Fiber: **4.0g**

TROPICAL COTTAGE CHEESE REFRESHER

Prep time: **5 minutes** | Cook time: **none** | Serves **1**

- 1 cup frozen pineapple chunks
- ½ cup fresh mango, chopped (about half a medium mango)
- ¼ cup 2% milkfat cottage cheese
- ½ cup 100% orange juice
- ¼ cup unsweetened coconut milk (from a carton, not canned)
- 1 tablespoon fresh lime juice
- ½ teaspoon lime zest (optional)

1. Add frozen pineapple, mango, cottage cheese, orange juice, coconut milk, lime juice, and lime zest (if using) to a blender.
2. Blend on high until smooth and creamy, about 1 minute.
3. Pour into a tall glass and serve immediately.
4. Chef's Tip: For a vacation-worthy presentation, garnish with a pineapple wedge and a small paper umbrella. To make it more filling, add a tablespoon of chia seeds or ground flaxseed.

Per Serving

Calories: **260** | Fat: **6.0g** | Protein: **10.0g** | Carbs: **45.0g** | Fiber: **5.0g**

CHOCOLATE PEANUT BUTTER POWER SMOOTHIE

Prep time: **5 minutes** | Cook time: **none** | Serves **1**

- 1 medium ripe banana (fresh or frozen)
- 2 tablespoons natural peanut butter (no added sugar)
- ¼ cup 2% milkfat cottage cheese
- 1 cup unsweetened almond milk
- 1 tablespoon unsweetened cocoa powder
- 1 tablespoon pure maple syrup
- ½ teaspoon vanilla extract (optional)
- 4-5 ice cubes (if using fresh banana)

1. Add banana, peanut butter, cottage cheese, almond milk, cocoa powder, maple syrup, vanilla extract (if using), and ice cubes (if using) to a blender.
2. Blend on high until smooth and creamy, about 45-60 seconds.
3. Pour into a glass and serve immediately.
4. Chef's Tip: For an extra protein boost, add a scoop of chocolate protein powder and reduce the cocoa powder to 1 teaspoon. You can substitute almond butter for peanut butter for a different flavor profile.

Per Serving

Calories: **350** | Fat: **18.0g** | Protein: **18.0g** | Carbs: **38.0g** | Fiber: **7.0g**

RASPBERRY-OAT BREAKFAST SMOOTHIE

Prep time: **5 minutes** | Cook time: **none** | Serves **1**

- 1 cup frozen raspberries
- ½ cup old-fashioned rolled oats
- ¼ cup 2% milkfat cottage cheese
- 1 cup milk (dairy or non-dairy of choice)
- 1 tablespoon chia seeds
- 1 tablespoon honey
- ¼ teaspoon cinnamon (optional)

1. Add frozen raspberries, rolled oats, cottage cheese, milk, chia seeds, honey, and cinnamon (if using) to a high-speed blender.
2. Blend on high until completely smooth and no oat pieces remain, about 60-90 seconds. If needed, stop and scrape down the sides of the blender.
3. Pour into a glass and serve immediately.
4. Chef's Tip: For a thicker, more filling smoothie, soak the oats and chia seeds in the milk for 10-15 minutes before blending. Add a handful of spinach for extra nutrients without affecting the taste.

Per Serving

Calories: **320** | Fat: **8.0g** | Protein: **16.0g** | Carbs: **48.0g** | Fiber: **8.0g**

STRAWBERRY-BANANA BLISS SMOOTHIE

Prep time: **5 minutes** | Cook time: **none** | Serves **1**

- ½ cup unsweetened almond milk
- ½ cup 2% milkfat cottage cheese
- ½ cup 2% Greek yogurt
- 1 medium ripe banana
- ½ cup fresh strawberries, hulled and halved, plus more for garnish
- 1 tablespoon ground flaxseeds
- 1 tablespoon honey or date paste
- ½ teaspoon pure vanilla extract
- 3-4 ice cubes (optional)

1. Add almond milk, cottage cheese, yogurt, banana, strawberries, flaxseeds, honey, vanilla extract, and ice cubes (if using) to a blender.
2. Blend on high speed until completely smooth and creamy, about 45-60 seconds.
3. Pour into a tall glass, garnish with sliced strawberries on top or along the rim of the glass, and serve immediately.
4. Chef's Tip: For a colder, thicker smoothie, use a frozen banana instead of fresh. You can prep ahead by freezing sliced

bananas and strawberries in individual portion bags for quick morning smoothies.

Per Serving

Calories: **260** | Fat: **6.5g** | Protein: **18.2g** | Carbs: **35.0g** | Fiber: **4.2g**

PEACHY VANILLA PROTEIN SHAKE

Prep time: **5 minutes** | Cook time: **none** | Serves **1**

- ½ cup unsweetened oat milk
- ½ cup 2% milkfat cottage cheese
- ¼ cup 2% Greek yogurt
- ½ cup frozen peach slices
- 1 tablespoon chia seeds
- 1 tablespoon pure maple syrup
- ½ teaspoon pure vanilla extract
- ¼ teaspoon ground cinnamon
- Dash of nutmeg (optional)

1. Add oat milk, cottage cheese, yogurt, frozen peaches, chia seeds, maple syrup, vanilla extract, cinnamon, and nutmeg (if using) to a blender.
2. Blend on high until completely smooth and creamy, about 45-60 seconds.
3. Pour into a glass and serve immediately.
4. Chef's Tip: Fresh peaches can be substituted when in season - just add 3-4 ice cubes to maintain the shake's chill and thickness. For extra protein, add a

scoop of vanilla protein powder.

Per Serving

Calories: **235** | Fat: **5.3g** | Protein: **17.1g** | Carbs: **30.4g** | Fiber: **5.0g**

BERRY VANILLA COTTAGE CHEESE BLAST

Prep time: **5 minutes** | Cook time: **none** | Serves **1**

- ¾ cup unsweetened almond milk
- ½ cup 2% milkfat cottage cheese
- 1 cup frozen mixed berries (strawberries, blueberries, raspberries)
- ½ teaspoon vanilla extract
- 1 tablespoon maple syrup (or other sweetener to taste)
- 1 tablespoon almond butter
- ¼ cup rolled oats
- 3-4 ice cubes (optional)

1. Toss the almond milk, cottage cheese, frozen berries, vanilla extract, maple syrup, almond butter, rolled oats, and ice cubes (if you're using 'em) into a blender.
2. Whiz it all up on high until it's totally smooth and creamy, should take about 45-60 seconds.
3. Pour it in a glass and enjoy right away!
4. Chef's Tip: Adding the almond butter and oats not only helps get those calories up but also adds a nice creaminess and a bit more staying power. If you

want an even bigger calorie boost, you could add a bit of flaxseed or chia seeds too!

Per Serving

Calories: **290** | Fat: **12.0g** | Protein: **21.5g** | Carbs: **31.0g** | Fiber: **5.3g**

MANGO-TURMERIC IMMUNITY SMOOTHIE

Prep time: **5 minutes** | Cook time: **none** | Serves **1**

- ½ cup coconut water
- ½ cup 2% milkfat cottage cheese
- ½ cup frozen mango chunks
- 1 tablespoon ground flaxseeds
- 1 tablespoon honey or date paste
- ½ teaspoon ground turmeric
- ¼ teaspoon freshly ground black pepper
- ½ teaspoon fresh lime juice
- Small piece of fresh ginger (about ½ inch), peeled (optional)

1. Add coconut water, cottage cheese, mango, flaxseeds, honey, turmeric, black pepper, lime juice, and fresh ginger (if using) to a blender.
2. Blend on high until completely smooth, about 45-60 seconds.
3. Pour into a glass and serve immediately.
4. Chef's Tip: The black pepper significantly increases the absorption of turmeric's anti-inflammatory compounds. For extra immune support, add ¼ teaspoon of ground cinnamon and a squeeze of orange juice. Frozen pineapple can be substituted for mango.

Per Serving

Calories: **220** | Fat: **3.8g** | Protein: **17.0g** | Carbs: **32.0g** | Fiber: **4.5g**

BERRY-ALMOND BREAKFAST SHAKE

Prep time: **5 minutes** | Cook time: **none** | Serves **1**

- ½ cup unsweetened almond milk
- ½ cup 2% milkfat cottage cheese
- ¼ cup 2% Greek yogurt
- ½ cup mixed berries (blueberries, raspberries, strawberries), fresh or frozen
- 1 tablespoon almond butter
- 1 tablespoon honey or date paste
- ¼ teaspoon almond extract
- 1 teaspoon lemon zest (optional)
- 3-4 ice cubes (if using fresh berries)

1. Add almond milk, cottage cheese, yogurt, mixed berries, almond butter, honey, almond extract, lemon zest (if using), and ice cubes (if using) to a blender.
2. Blend on high until smooth and creamy, about 45-60 seconds.
3. Pour into a glass and serve immediately.
4. Chef's Tip: For a beautiful layered effect, blend the berries separately with half the liquid ingredients, pour into your glass, then blend the remaining ingredients and pour on top. Use a

straw or spoon to create a slight marbled effect before serving.

Per Serving

Calories: **245** | Fat: **8.5g** | Protein: **18.8g** | Carbs: **29.5g** | Fiber: **4.8g**

CHAPTER 5: PROTEIN-BOOSTED SALADS

SPECIAL CHICKEN SALAD

Prep time: 5 minutes | Cook time: 15 minutes |Serves 3

- 1 boneless, skinless chicken breast (about 6 ounces)
- ¼ cup mayonnaise
- ¼ cup sour cream
- 2 tablespoons cottage cheese, at room temperature
- Salt and freshly ground black pepper, to taste
- ¼ cup roasted, hulled sunflower seeds
- ½ avocado, peeled and cubed
- ½ teaspoon minced fresh garlic
- 2 tablespoons chopped scallions (green onions)

1. Bring a medium pot of well-salted water to a rolling boil.
2. Carefully add the chicken breast to the boiling water. Turn off the heat, cover the pot, and let the chicken stand in the hot water for 15 minutes, or until cooked through.
3. Drain the water and let the chicken cool slightly. Once cool enough to handle, chop the chicken into bite-sized pieces.
4. In a medium bowl, combine the chopped chicken, mayonnaise, sour cream, cottage cheese, salt, pepper, sunflower seeds, avocado, garlic, and scallions. Mix thoroughly.

5. Cover the bowl and refrigerate for at least one hour to allow the flavors to meld. Serve chilled.

Per Serving

Calories: **411** | Fat: **35.1g** | Carbs: **5.6g** | Fiber: **2.9g** | Protein: **16.1g**

GREEK COTTAGE CHEESE SALAD

Prep time: 5 minutes | Cook time: 5 minutes |Serves 2

- 4 cups baby spinach leaves
- 4 tablespoons Kalamata olives, pitted and sliced
- 1 small red onion, thinly sliced
- 1 small cucumber, halved and sliced
- ½ cup cherry tomatoes, halved
- 1 cup 2% cottage cheese
- 2 tablespoons extra virgin olive oil
- 2 tablespoons red wine vinegar
- 2 teaspoons dried oregano
- Juice of 1 lemon
- Salt, to taste

- Freshly ground black pepper, to taste
- ½ cup crumbled feta cheese (optional for extra flavor and calories)
- ½ cup cooked quinoa (optional for extra protein and fiber)

1. In a large bowl, combine the spinach, olives, red onion, cucumber, cherry tomatoes, cottage cheese, feta (if using), and quinoa (if using).
2. In a small bowl, whisk together the olive oil, red wine vinegar, oregano, lemon juice, salt, and pepper.
3. Drizzle the dressing over

the salad, toss gently to combine, and serve immediately.

Per Serving

Calorie: **520** | Fat: **34g** | Carbs: **27g** | Protein: **32g** | Fiber: **9g**

PERFECT PROTEIN SALAD WITH BUTTERMILK DRESSING

Prep time: **20 minutes** | Cook time: **none** | Serves **1**

- 2 cups baby spring mix
- 2 scallions (green onions), chopped
- 1 small cucumber, halved and sliced
- 4 white button mushrooms, halved and sliced
- ¼ medium avocado, peeled and chopped
- ½ cup 2% cottage cheese
- 1 hard-boiled egg, peeled and chopped
- 3 tablespoons low-fat buttermilk
- Juice of 1 lemon

- 1 clove garlic, minced
- Salt, to taste
- Freshly ground black pepper, to taste

1. In a medium bowl, combine the spring mix, scallions, cucumber, mushrooms, avocado, cottage cheese, and chopped hard-boiled egg.
2. In a small bowl, whisk together the buttermilk, lemon juice, minced garlic, salt, and pepper.
3. Drizzle the buttermilk dressing over the salad, toss gently to coat, and serve immediately.

Per Serving

Calorie: **349** | Fat: **24g** | Carbs: **18g** | Protein: **24g** | Fiber: **8g**

"BIG MAC" INSPIRED COTTAGE CHEESE SALAD

Prep time: **10 minutes** | Cook time: **9 minutes** | Serves **2**

- 4 cups chopped romaine lettuce
- ½ cup dill pickle slices
- 8 ounces ground beef (80/20 blend)
- 2 scallions (green onions), chopped
- ½ cup shredded Monterey Jack cheese
- 1 tablespoon sesame oil
- 2 tablespoons heavy cream
- 1 teaspoon ground black pepper

Dressing:
- ½ cup cottage cheese
- 2 tablespoons mayonnaise
- 1 tablespoon yellow mustard
- 1 tablespoon pickle juice
- 1 teaspoon paprika

- ½ teaspoon garlic powder
- ¼ teaspoon onion powder
- Salt and pepper to taste.

1. In a bowl, combine the ground beef and black pepper. Form into small patties (mini burgers).
2. Heat the sesame oil in a skillet or Instant Pot (using the sauté function) over medium-high heat.
3. Cook the mini burgers for 3 minutes per side, or until cooked through.
4. While the burgers are cooking, in a large salad bowl, combine the chopped romaine lettuce, dill pickle slices, scallions, and shredded Monterey Jack cheese.
5. In a small bowl combine all dressing ingredients, and blend with an immersion blender, or food processor until smooth.
6. Toss the salad with the dressing, and top with the cooked mini burgers. Serve immediately.

Per Serving

Calories: **284** | Fat: **18.5g** | Fiber: **1.2g** | Carbs: **3.5g** | Protein: **25.7g**

PORK CHOPS AND ROASTED WINTER SQUASH SALAD

Prep time: **10 minutes** | Cook time: **35 minutes** | Serves **6**

- 4 boneless pork chops (about 1 inch thick)
- 2 tablespoons grapeseed oil, divided
- ½ teaspoon sea salt
- ¼ teaspoon ground black pepper
- ½ teaspoon paprika
- ½ teaspoon garlic powder
- 1 teaspoon shallot powder
- 1 teaspoon dried parsley flakes
- 1 cup water
- 1 cup winter squash (butternut or acorn), diced
- 1 head iceberg lettuce, chopped
- 1 cucumber, sliced
- 3 ounces feta cheese, crumbled
- ½ cup cottage cheese.

1. Press the "Sauté" button on the Instant Pot to heat. Add 1 tablespoon of grapeseed oil and brown the pork chops for 2 minutes per side.
2. Add salt, black pepper, paprika, garlic powder, shallot powder, parsley flakes, and water to the Instant Pot.
3. Secure the lid. Choose "Manual" or "Pressure Cook" mode and cook for 8 minutes under high pressure. Perform a quick pressure release and carefully remove the lid.
4. Meanwhile, preheat your oven to 390°F. Toss the diced winter squash with the remaining 1 tablespoon of grapeseed oil. Spread the squash on a lightly greased baking sheet and bake for 18 minutes, or until tender. Allow it to cool completely.
5. In a large salad bowl, combine the cooked and cooled winter squash,

chopped iceberg lettuce, sliced cucumber, and cottage cheese.
6. Mound the salad onto individual serving plates. Top with the cooked pork chops and scatter crumbled feta cheese over each serving. Enjoy.

Per Serving

Calories: 380 | Fat: 25g | Carbs: 15g | Protein: 28g | Fiber: 3g

CREAMY COTTAGE CHEESE SHRIMP SALAD

Prep time: **10 minutes** | Cook time: **10 minutes** | Serves **4**

- 28 ounces shrimp, peeled and deveined
- ½ cup apple cider vinegar
- ½ cup water
- ⅓ cup mayonnaise
- ¼ cup cottage cheese
- 1 celery stalk with leaves, chopped
- ½ medium red onion, chopped
- 1 large cucumber, sliced
- 1 tablespoon lime juice
- 2 tablespoons chopped fresh cilantro

1. Toss the shrimp, apple cider vinegar, and water in the Instant Pot.
2. Secure the lid. Choose "Manual" or "Pressure Cook" mode on low pressure; cook for 2 minutes. Perform a quick pressure release and carefully remove the lid.
3. Drain the shrimp and allow them to cool completely.
4. In a large bowl, gently combine the cooled shrimp, mayonnaise, cottage cheese, chopped celery, red onion, cucumber slices, lime juice, and chopped cilantro. Mix well.

5. Chill for at least 30 minutes before serving.

Per Serving

Calories: 261 | Fat: 18g | Carbs: 8g | Protein: 22g | Fiber: 2g

SHREDDED CHICKEN AND CABBAGE SALAD

Prep time: **10 minutes** | Cook time: **12 minutes** | Serves **4**

- 9 ounces napa cabbage, shredded
- 10 ounces boneless, skinless chicken breast
- ½ teaspoon lemon juice
- ¼ cup heavy cream
- 1 teaspoon white pepper
- ½ cup water
- ½ teaspoon salt
- ½ teaspoon ground turmeric
- ¼ teaspoon dried sage
- 1 tablespoon cream cheese, softened
- 1 tablespoon sour cream
- ½ teaspoon dried dill
- ¼ cup cottage cheese (added for protein boost)

1. Rub the chicken breast with white pepper, salt, ground turmeric, and dried sage. Place it in the Instant Pot. Add water and heavy cream. Close and seal the lid. Cook the chicken on "Manual" or "Pressure Cook" mode (high pressure) for 12 minutes. Then, perform a quick pressure release.

2. Remove the chicken breast from the Instant Pot and shred it using two forks. Put the shredded chicken in a large salad bowl.

3. In the Instant Pot (with the remaining cream mixture), add the sour cream, cream cheese, cottage cheese, and dill. Stir until well combined and smooth.

4. Sprinkle the shredded

chicken and cabbage with lemon juice and pour half of the cream mixture from the Instant Pot over it. Toss the salad well. Serve immediately, or chill for later.

Per Serving

Calories: **187** | Fat: **9.7g** | Fiber: **0.9g** | Carbs: **2.4g** | Protein: **22g**

SIMPLE STEAMED TOMATO COTTAGE CHEESE SALAD

Prep time: **10 minutes** | Cook time: **10 minutes** | Serves **4**

- 1 cup water
- 8 medium tomatoes, sliced
- 2 tablespoons extra-virgin olive oil
- ½ cup crumbled cottage cheese
- 2 garlic cloves, smashed
- 2 tablespoons fresh basil, snipped

1. Pour 1 cup of water into the bottom of an Instant Pot. Place a steamer basket or

rack inside.

2. Arrange the sliced tomatoes on the steamer rack.

3. Secure the lid. Choose "Manual" or "Pressure Cook" mode on high pressure and cook for 3 minutes. Perform a quick pressure release and carefully remove the lid.

4. Transfer the steamed tomatoes to a serving bowl. Add the olive oil, crumbled cottage cheese, smashed garlic, and snipped basil. Gently toss to combine. Serve warm or at room temperature.

Per Serving

Calories: **168** | Fat: **10g** | Carbs: **8g** | Protein: **6g** | Fiber: **2g**

CHICKEN AND LETTUCE SALAD WITH COTTAGE CHEESE DRESSING

Prep time: **10 minutes** | Cook time: **15 minutes** | Serves **2**

- 1 garlic clove
- ½ teaspoon anchovy paste
- Juice of ½ lemon
- 2 tablespoons olive oil
- 1 (8-ounce) boneless, skinless chicken breast
- ¼ teaspoon salt
- Black pepper, to taste
- 2 romaine lettuce hearts, cored and chopped
- 1 red bell pepper, julienned
- ¼ cup grated Parmesan cheese

Dressing:

- ½ cup Cottage cheese
- 2 tablespoons water
- 1 tablespoon lemon juice
- 1 garlic clove
- ¼ teaspoon black pepper.

1. Preheat the broiler to high.
2. For the dressing, combine cottage cheese, water, lemon juice, garlic, and black pepper in a blender and blend until smooth.
3. Cut the chicken breast lengthwise into 2 even cutlets.
4. Season the chicken with salt and pepper. Place on a baking sheet.
5. Broil the chicken for 5-7 minutes per side, until cooked through and browned.
6. In a large bowl, toss the lettuce, bell pepper, and Parmesan cheese.

7. Add the cottage cheese dressing and toss to coat.
8. Divide the salad between two plates and top with the cooked chicken. Serve immediately.

Per Serving

Calories: 392 | **Carbs: 6g** | **Proteins: 28g** | **Fats: 18g** | **Fiber: 2g**

TYROLEAN COTTAGE CHEESE EGG SALAD

Prep time: **10 minutes** | Cook time: **20 minutes** | Serves **4**

- 6 large eggs
- ½ pound green beans, trimmed
- 1 cup water, divided
- 3 slices prosciutto, chopped
- ½ cup green onions, chopped
- 1 carrot, shredded
- ½ cup mayonnaise
- 1 tablespoon apple cider vinegar
- 1 teaspoon yellow mustard
- 4 ounces Gorgonzola cheese, crumbled
- ½ cup cottage cheese

1. Pour ½ cup of water into the Instant Pot. Place a steamer basket inside. Arrange the eggs in the steamer basket.

2. Secure the lid. Choose "Manual" or "Pressure Cook" mode on high pressure and cook for 5 minutes. Perform a natural pressure release (about 10 minutes) and carefully remove the lid.
3. Allow the eggs to cool for 15 minutes. Peel and slice them.
4. Pour the remaining ½ cup of water into the Instant Pot. Add the green beans.
5. Secure the lid. Choose "Manual" or "Pressure Cook" mode on low pressure and cook for 5 minutes. Perform a quick pressure release and carefully remove the lid.
6. Transfer the green beans to a large salad bowl. Add the chopped prosciutto, green onions, shredded carrot, mayonnaise, vinegar,

mustard, and cottage cheese.

7. Gently toss to combine.
8. Top with the sliced eggs and crumbled Gorgonzola cheese. Serve immediately, or chill for later.

Per Serving

Calories: 380 | **Fat: 30g** | **Carbs: 8g** | **Protein: 20g** | **Fiber: 2g**

CHAPTER 6: PROTEIN-FORWARD MAIN DISHES

TURKEY AND COTTAGE CHEESE BAKE

Prep time: **10 minutes** | Cook time: **40 minutes** | Serves **4**

- 1 tablespoon vegetable oil
- 1 pound boneless, skinless turkey thighs, cubed into 1-inch pieces
- 8 ounces smoked deli ham, diced
- 8 ounces cottage cheese (full-fat, small curd recommended)
- ½ teaspoon dry mustard powder
- ¼ teaspoon cayenne pepper, or more to taste
- 1 cup low-sodium chicken broth
- 2 cups shredded Gruyère cheese
- Salt and freshly ground black pepper, to taste
- 2 tablespoons fresh chives, chopped (for garnish)

1. Press the "Sauté" button to heat up the Instant Pot. Add the oil and cook the turkey thighs until no longer pink, about 5-7 minutes, stirring occasionally.
2. Add ham, cottage cheese, mustard powder, cayenne pepper, and chicken broth; gently stir to combine.
3. Secure the lid and set the valve to the sealing position. Select the "Meat/Stew" setting and cook for 35 minutes at High pressure.
4. Once cooking is complete, allow for a natural pressure release (about 10-15 minutes), then carefully remove the lid.
5. Stir in the shredded Gruyère cheese and continue to

cook in the residual heat until the cheese has melted completely, about 2-3 minutes.
6. Season with salt and black pepper to taste. Garnish with fresh chives before serving.

Per Serving

Calories: **580** | Fat: **45g** | Carbs: **6g** | Protein: **40g** | Fiber: **1g**

CHEESY BEEF AND CAULIFLOWER SKILLET

Prep time: **10 minutes** | Cook time: **25 minutes** | Serves **4**

- 1 ½ tablespoons olive oil
- 1 pound beef chuck, cut into ½-inch cubes
- Kosher salt, to taste
- 2 garlic cloves, minced
- 1 medium leek, white and light green parts only, chopped
- 2 cups cauliflower florets, chopped
- 1 cup celery, diced
- ½ teaspoon dried rosemary
- ½ teaspoon red pepper flakes
- Freshly ground black pepper, to taste
- 8 ounces cottage cheese, room temperature
- 1 cup shredded cheddar cheese
- 4 strips bacon, cooked and crumbled
- 2 tablespoons fresh parsley, chopped

1. Heat a large skillet over medium-high heat and add the olive oil. Sear the beef until browned on all sides, about 5 minutes. Season with salt and transfer to a plate.
2. In the same skillet, add the garlic and leek; sauté for 2-3 minutes until fragrant and softened.
3. Return the beef to the skillet. Add the cauliflower, celery, rosemary, red pepper flakes, and black pepper. Stir to combine.
4. Reduce the heat to medium-low, cover, and cook for about 15 minutes, stirring occasionally, until the cauliflower is tender and most of the moisture has reduced.

5. Stir in the cottage cheese and cheddar cheese, cooking until fully melted and combined, creating a thick, creamy texture.
6. Remove from heat and top with crumbled bacon and fresh parsley. Serve hot.

Per Serving

Calories: **523** | Fat: **38g** | Carbs: **14g** | Protein: **35g** | Fiber: **4g**

LOADED COTTAGE CHEESE BROCCOLI BAKED POTATOES

Prep time: 5 minutes | **Cook time: 45 minutes to 1 hour** | **Serves 2**

- 2 large russet potatoes (about 12 ounces each)
- 2 teaspoons olive oil
- 2 teaspoons kosher salt
- 2 cups small broccoli florets
- ¼ teaspoon salt
- 2 tablespoons unsalted butter, divided
- 1 ½ cups low-fat cottage cheese (2%), divided
- 2 tablespoons fresh chives, chopped, divided
- ¼ cup shredded sharp cheddar cheese (optional)
- Freshly ground black pepper, to taste

1. Preheat the oven to 400°F. Thoroughly wash and scrub the potato skins. Pat dry, then pierce each potato with a fork several times on all sides. Rub the potatoes with olive oil and sprinkle with kosher salt.
2. Place potatoes directly onto the middle oven rack and bake for 45-60 minutes, until the skin is crisp and the inside is soft when pierced with a fork.
3. While potatoes are baking, bring a medium pot of water to a boil. Add a pinch of salt and the broccoli florets. Blanch for 30-45 seconds until bright green. Immediately drain and transfer to a bowl of ice water for 5 minutes. Drain well and set aside.
4. When the potatoes are done, carefully remove them from the oven using tongs.
5. Let the potatoes cool slightly, then cut them in half lengthwise. Gently fluff the insides with a fork.
6. Top each potato half with ½ tablespoon butter, ½ cup broccoli florets, and 3/4 cup cottage cheese. If using cheddar cheese, sprinkle 2 tablespoons over each potato. Garnish with chives and season with freshly ground black pepper.
7. For meal prep: Allow potatoes to cool completely before placing in airtight containers. Refrigerate for up to 3 days.

Per Serving

Calories: 405 | **Fat: 26g** | **Protein: 30g** | **Carbs: 46g** | **Fiber: 8g**

CREAMY COTTAGE CHEESE MAC AND CHEESE

Prep time: **10 minutes** | Cook time: **25 minutes** | Serves **6**

- 1 cup fat-free evaporated milk
- ½ cup skim milk
- ½ cup reduced-fat sharp cheddar cheese, shredded
- 1 cup cottage cheese (small curd)
- ¼ teaspoon ground nutmeg
- 1/8 teaspoon cayenne pepper
- ½ teaspoon salt
- ¼ teaspoon freshly ground black pepper
- 6 cups cooked whole-wheat elbow macaroni (about 3 cups dry)
- 2 tablespoons grated Parmesan cheese
- 1 tablespoon whole wheat breadcrumbs (optional)
- 1 tablespoon fresh parsley, chopped (for garnish)

1. Preheat the oven to 350°F. Coat a 9x13-inch baking dish with cooking spray.
2. In a large saucepan, heat both milks over medium-low heat until steaming but not boiling, about 3-4 minutes.
3. Reduce heat to low and gradually add the cheddar cheese and cottage cheese, whisking constantly until the cheese is fully melted and the mixture is smooth, about 5 minutes.
4. Season with nutmeg, cayenne pepper, salt, and black pepper, stirring well to combine.
5. Remove from heat. Add the cooked macaroni to the cheese sauce and fold gently until well coated.
6. Transfer the macaroni and cheese mixture to the prepared baking dish. Spread evenly and top with the grated Parmesan cheese

and breadcrumbs if using.
7. Bake for 20-25 minutes, or until the top is lightly golden brown and the edges are bubbly.
8. Let stand for 5 minutes before serving. Garnish with fresh parsley if desired.

Per Serving

Calories: **245** | Fat: **2.1g** | Protein: **15.7g** | Carbs: **43.8g** | Fiber: **3.8g**

TROPICAL COTTAGE CHEESE BOWL

Prep time: **5 minutes** | Cook time: **15 minutes** | Serves **3**

- 2¼ cups (18 oz) reduced-fat cottage cheese (2%), divided
- 1½ cups fresh pineapple chunks, divided
- ¾ cup diced fresh mango or additional pineapple, divided
- ¾ teaspoon ground cinnamon, divided
- 3 tablespoons honey or maple syrup (optional), divided
- 3 tablespoons roasted slivered almonds, divided
- 3 tablespoons low-sugar granola (optional), divided
- Fresh mint leaves for garnish (optional)

1. For meal prep: Divide the ingredients among 3 airtight storage containers, placing ¾ cup cottage cheese, ½ cup pineapple, and ¼ cup mango in each container.
2. Sprinkle each portion with ¼ teaspoon cinnamon and drizzle with 1 tablespoon honey or maple syrup if desired.
3. Seal the containers and refrigerate for up to 3 days.
4. Just before eating, top each serving with 1 tablespoon each of almonds and granola (if using) for added

crunch.
5. Garnish with fresh mint if desired.

Per Serving

Calories: **254** | Fat: **7g** | Protein: **25g** | Carbs: **25g** | Fiber: **3g**

LENTIL AND ZUCCHINI PASTA BAKE

Prep time: 10 minutes | Cook time: 20 minutes | Serves 4

- 2 cups dry whole-grain pasta
- 2 tablespoons extra-virgin olive oil
- 4 small zucchini (about 1 pound), coarsely chopped
- 1 (8-ounce) container sliced mushrooms
- 1 large yellow onion, chopped
- 1 medium green bell pepper, seeded and chopped
- 2 (15-ounce) cans lentils, drained
- 1 (15-ounce) can diced tomatoes
- 1 cup reduced-fat cottage cheese
- ½ teaspoon dried oregano
- ½ teaspoon dried basil
- ½ teaspoon salt
- ¼ teaspoon freshly ground black pepper
- 1 cup shredded mozzarella cheese

1. Preheat the oven to 350°F.
2. Bring a large pot of water to a boil over high heat and cook the pasta according to the package directions. Drain and set aside.
3. Meanwhile, in a large skillet over medium-high heat, heat the oil. Sauté the zucchini, mushrooms, onion, and bell pepper for about 10 minutes, until softened.
4. Add the lentils, tomatoes with their juice, cottage cheese, oregano, basil, salt, and pepper. Mix in the cooked pasta and transfer to a 9×13-inch baking dish.
5. Sprinkle evenly with the mozzarella and bake for about 10 minutes, until the cheese is melted and bubbly.

Per Serving

Calories: 496 | Fat: 15g | Carbs: 60g | Protein: 25g | Fiber: 12g

MEDITERRANEAN FISH AND COTTAGE CHEESE BAKE

Prep time: 10 minutes | Cook time: 15 minutes | Serves 4

- Nonstick cooking spray
- 2 ripe tomatoes, sliced
- 1 teaspoon dried basil
- 1 teaspoon dried oregano
- ½ teaspoon dried rosemary
- 2 cloves garlic, minced
- 1 head cauliflower, cut into florets
- 1 red onion, sliced
- 1 pound tilapia fillets, sliced
- Sea salt, to taste
- 1 tablespoon olive oil
- 1 cup cottage cheese
- 1/3 cup Kalamata olives, pitted and halved

1. Add 1½ cups of water and a metal trivet to the bottom of your Instant Pot.
2. Generously coat a 7-inch round casserole dish with nonstick cooking spray. Arrange the tomato slices on the bottom of the dish. Sprinkle with the basil, oregano, rosemary, and garlic.
3. Layer the cauliflower and onion on top, then arrange the sliced fish over the vegetables. Season with sea salt and drizzle with olive oil.
4. Spread the cottage cheese evenly over the fish and top with Kalamata olives. Lower the casserole dish onto the trivet in the Instant Pot.
5. Secure the lid. Select "Manual" or "Pressure Cook" mode on High pressure; cook for 5 minutes. Once cooking is complete, perform a quick pressure release and carefully remove the lid.
6. Allow the dish to rest for 5 minutes before serving. Enjoy!

Per Serving

Calories: 372 | Fat: 15g | Carbs: 18g | Protein: 38g | Fiber: 5g

GROUND PORK TACO CASSEROLE

Prep time: 10 minutes | Cook time: 35 minutes | Serves 6

- 8 ounces cottage cheese, at room temperature
- ¼ cup heavy cream
- 2 large eggs
- 1 teaspoon taco seasoning, plus 1 tablespoon (divided)
- ¾ pound ground pork
- ½ cup tomato sauce
- 1 (4-ounce) can chopped green chilies
- 1½ cups Mexican blend shredded cheese, divided

1. Add 1½ cups of water and a metal trivet to the bottom of your Instant Pot.
2. In a mixing bowl, thoroughly combine cottage cheese, heavy cream, eggs, and 1 teaspoon taco seasoning.
3. Lightly grease a 7-inch round casserole dish that fits in your Instant Pot. Spread ½ cup of the Mexican blend cheese over the bottom. Pour the cottage cheese/egg mixture over it as evenly as possible.
4. Lower the casserole dish onto the trivet in the Instant Pot.
5. Secure the lid. Select "Manual" or "Pressure Cook" mode on High pressure; cook for 20 minutes. Once cooking is complete, perform a quick pressure release; carefully remove the lid.
6. Meanwhile, heat a cast-iron skillet over medium-high heat. Brown the ground pork, breaking it up with a fork as it cooks.
7. Add the remaining tablespoon of taco seasoning, tomato sauce, and green chilies. Stir to combine.
8. Spread this meat mixture over the cooked cheese and egg layer.
9. Top with the remaining 1 cup of Mexican blend cheese.
10. Return the casserole to the Instant Pot, secure the lid, and select "Manual" or "Pressure Cook" mode on High pressure; cook for 10 minutes. Once cooking is complete, perform a quick pressure release and carefully remove the lid.
11. Let stand for 5 minutes before serving.

Per Serving

Calories: 409 | Fat: 32g | Carbs: 6g | Protein: 28g | Fiber: 1g

FILET MIGNON WITH CARAMELIZED ONIONS

Prep time: **10 minutes** | Cook time: **15 minutes** | Serves **3**

- 3 filet mignon steaks (about 6 ounces each)
- ¼ cup olive oil
- 1 tablespoon Dijon mustard
- ¼ cup aged balsamic vinegar
- 2 cups onions, sliced medium-thick
- ½ cup cottage cheese, drained
- 1 tablespoon butter
- 1 teaspoon sugar
- 2 teaspoons dried rosemary
- Freshly cracked black pepper
- Seasoned salt

1. Generously season the steaks with cracked black pepper and seasoned salt, then place them in a dish in a single layer.
2. In a medium bowl, whisk together the balsamic vinegar, olive oil, rosemary, and Dijon mustard until well combined. Pour this marinade over the filets, coating both sides. Cover the dish with plastic wrap and refrigerate to marinate for 30 minutes.
3. Meanwhile, select "Sauté" function on your Instant Pot and add the butter. When melted, add the onion slices and sugar. Cook for about 5 minutes, stirring occasionally, until the onions become caramelized and golden brown.
4. Remove the onions and set aside. Add the marinated steaks to the Instant Pot (still on "Sauté" function) and cook for about 2-3 minutes per side for medium-rare, or to your desired doneness.
5. Top each steak with caramelized onions and 2-3 tablespoons of cottage cheese. Select "Manual" or "Pressure Cook" on Low pressure for 1 minute just to warm the cottage cheese.
6. Perform a quick pressure release, carefully remove the lid, and serve the steaks immediately.

Per Serving

Calories: **511** | Fat: **42g** | Carbs: **16g** | Protein: **40g** | Fiber: **2g**

CHAPTER 7: PROTEIN-ENRICHED PASTA AND PIZZA

STUFFED PASTA SHELLS WITH COTTAGE CHEESE

Prep time: **30 minutes** | Cook time: **55 minutes** | Serves **5**

- 15 uncooked jumbo pasta shells
- ½ pound lean (at least 90%) ground turkey
- 1 teaspoon dried Italian seasoning
- ½ teaspoon fennel seed
- ¼ teaspoon black pepper
- 2 cups fresh mushrooms, sliced
- 1 medium onion, chopped (½ cup)
- 4 cloves garlic, finely chopped
- 1 cup fat-free cottage cheese
- ¼ cup liquid egg substitute (or 2 egg whites)
- 2 cups tomato pasta sauce
- ¼ cup Parmesan cheese, shredded

1. Heat oven to 350°F. Cook and drain pasta as directed on package, omitting salt.
2. Meanwhile, in a 10-inch nonstick skillet, cook turkey, Italian seasoning, fennel and pepper over medium heat for 8 to 10 minutes, stirring occasionally, until turkey is no longer pink; remove turkey mixture from skillet.
3. In the same skillet, cook mushrooms, onion and garlic over medium heat for 6 to 8 minutes, stirring occasionally, until vegetables are tender. Stir turkey mixture, cottage cheese and egg substitute into mushroom mixture.
4. Spray a 13×9-inch (3-quart) glass baking dish with cooking spray. Spoon about 1 tablespoon of turkey

mixture into each pasta shell. Arrange shells in the baking dish. Spoon pasta sauce evenly over shells.

5. Cover with foil. Bake for 20 to 25 minutes or until hot and bubbly. Sprinkle with Parmesan cheese before serving.

Per Serving

Calories: **340** | Fat: **8g** | Carbs: **44g** | Fiber: **3g** | Protein: **23g**

BREAKFAST PIZZA WITH COTTAGE CHEESE

Prep time: **10 minutes** | Cook time: **5 minutes** | Serves **1**

- Nonstick cooking spray
- 4 slices turkey pepperoni
- 2 tablespoons green bell pepper, diced
- 2 tablespoons mushrooms, pre-sliced
- 2 egg whites
- 1 tablespoon low-fat milk
- 2 tablespoons cottage cheese
- 1 whole wheat sandwich thin or English muffin, split
- 2 teaspoons pizza sauce
- 1 slice part-skim mozzarella cheese
- 4 slices Roma tomato

1. Coat a small nonstick skillet with cooking spray and heat over medium heat. Add

pepperoni, mushrooms, and bell pepper to the skillet. Cook for about 2 minutes, stirring occasionally.

2. In a small bowl, whisk together the egg whites and milk, then pour over the pepperoni mixture in the skillet.
3. Cook until the egg whites begin to set. Fold the partially cooked egg white mixture over with a spatula; cook for another 2 minutes or until fully cooked.
4. Meanwhile, lightly toast the sandwich thin or English muffin halves.
5. Spread 1 teaspoon of pizza sauce on each half of the sandwich thin.
6. Spread 1 tablespoon of cottage cheese over each half.

7. Divide the egg mixture between the two halves.
8. Top each half with 2 slices of tomato and half of the mozzarella cheese slice.
9. Place under the broiler for 1-2 minutes until the cheese is melted and bubbly.

Per Serving

Calories: **218** | Carbs: **23.2** | Protein: **21g** | Fat: **6g** | Fiber: **3g**

CREAMY ITALIAN CHICKEN & PASTA

Prep time: **10 minutes**| Cook time: **20 minutes**| Serves **4**

- 2 boneless, skinless chicken breasts, cut in 1-inch pieces
- 1 cup half-and-half
- ¼ cup cottage cheese
- 1 cup baby spinach
- ¼ cup fresh basil, finely diced
- ¼ cup sun-dried tomatoes
- 8 ounces pasta, cooked and drained
- ½ cup dry white wine (or chicken broth)
- ¼ cup Parmesan cheese, grated
- 1 tablespoon olive oil
- 1 teaspoon all-purpose flour
- 1 teaspoon lemon juice
- ½ teaspoon Dijon mustard
- ¼ teaspoon garlic powder
- ¼ teaspoon Italian seasoning
- ¼ teaspoon smoked paprika
- Salt and pepper, to taste

1. Heat oil in a large skillet over medium-high heat. Add chicken and sprinkle with garlic powder, Italian seasoning, smoked paprika, salt, and pepper. Cook, stirring frequently, until chicken is no longer pink, about 5 minutes. Transfer to a plate.
2. Add wine (or broth), Dijon mustard, flour, and lemon juice to the skillet. Stir until combined and cook until mixture starts to bubble.
3. Add the sun-dried tomatoes and half-and-half to the pan. Let it simmer for 2 minutes.
4. Stir in the cottage cheese until well combined.
5. Add chicken back to the pan. Cook for another few minutes until the chicken is cooked through.
6. Stir in the basil and spinach. Let it cook for a minute or so until spinach wilts. Taste and season with extra salt and pepper if needed.
7. Add cooked pasta and toss to coat. Serve immediately with Parmesan cheese sprinkled over the top.

Per Serving

Calories: **316** |Carbs: **12g** | Protein: **25g** |Fat: **16g** | Fiber: **2g**

SAVORY LINGUINE WITH COTTAGE CHEESE PESTO

Prep time: **10 minutes** | Cook time: **20 minutes** | Serves **6**

- ½ cup shredded kale
- ½ cup fresh basil
- ½ cup sun-dried tomatoes
- ¼ cup chopped almonds
- 2 tablespoons extra-virgin olive oil
- ½ cup cottage cheese
- 8 ounces dry whole-wheat linguine
- ¼ cup grated Parmesan cheese

1. In a food processor or blender, combine the kale, basil, sun-dried tomatoes, almonds, cottage cheese, and olive oil. Pulse until a thick paste forms, about 2 minutes.
2. Place the pesto in a mixing bowl and set aside. Bring a large pot of water to a boil over high heat.
3. Cook the pasta until it is al dente, following package directions.
4. Drain the pasta and combine it with the pesto and Parmesan cheese in a large mixing bowl.

5. Serve immediately.

Per Serving

Calories: **218** | Fat: **10.1g** | Protein: **9.1g** | Carbs: **25.1g** | Fiber: **1.1g**

FLORENTINE COTTAGE CHEESE PIZZA

Prep time: **15 minutes** | Cook time: **20 minutes** | Serves **2**

- 1 cup shredded mozzarella cheese
- ¾ cup cottage cheese, well drained
- ½ cup frozen spinach, thawed
- 1 large egg
- 2 tablespoons grated Parmesan cheese
- 2 tablespoons cream cheese, softened
- ¾ cup almond flour
- ¼ cup light Alfredo sauce
- ½ teaspoon Italian seasoning
- ¼ teaspoon red pepper flakes
- Pinch of salt

1. Preheat oven to 400°F.

2. Squeeze all the excess water out of the spinach using a clean kitchen towel or paper towels.
3. In a microwave-safe bowl, combine 1 cup of mozzarella cheese, cream cheese, and almond flour. Microwave on high for 1 minute, then stir. If the mixture is not fully melted, microwave for another 30 seconds.
4. Stir in the egg, Italian seasoning, and salt. Mix well. Place dough on a piece of parchment paper and press into a 10-inch circle.
5. Place directly on the oven rack (with parchment paper) and bake for 8 to 10 minutes or until lightly browned.
6. Remove the crust and spread with the Alfredo sauce, then evenly distribute the drained cottage cheese, spinach, Parmesan cheese, and red pepper flakes over the top.
7. Bake for another 8 to 10 minutes. Slice and serve.

Per Serving

Calories: **442** | Fat: **35.0g** | Protein: **24.1g** | Carbs: **14.1g** | Fiber: **5.0g**

BBQ CHICKEN & NOODLES WITH COTTAGE CHEESE

Prep time: **10 minutes** | Cook time: **25 minutes** | Serves **4**

- 4 slices bacon, diced
- 1 boneless, skinless chicken breast (about 8 oz), cut into 1-inch pieces
- 1 onion, diced
- ½ cup cottage cheese
- ½ cup low-fat cheddar cheese, grated
- ½ cup milk (1% or 2%)
- 1 (14.5 oz) can diced tomatoes
- 2 cups low-sodium chicken broth
- ¼ cup barbecue sauce
- 2 cloves garlic, finely diced
- ¼ teaspoon red pepper flakes
- 8 ounces egg noodles

- Salt and pepper, to taste

1. Place a large pot over medium-high heat. Add bacon and cook until crispy. Drain fat, reserving 1 tablespoon in the pot.
2. Add chicken to the pot and cook until browned on all sides, 3-5 minutes.
3. Add garlic and onion and cook, stirring often, until onions are translucent, 3-4 minutes.
4. Stir in broth, tomatoes, milk, red pepper flakes, salt, and pepper. Bring to a boil, cover, reduce heat and simmer for 10 minutes.
5. Stir in barbecue sauce and egg noodles. Cook according to noodle package directions until al dente.
6. Just before serving, stir in cottage cheese and cheddar cheese until melted and well combined. Serve immediately.

Per Serving

Calories: **431** | Carbs: **18g** | Protein: **34g** | Fat: **13g** | Fiber: **3g**

CHICKEN & SPINACH SKILLET

Prep time: **10 minutes** | Cook time: **15 minutes** | Serves **4**

- 1 pound boneless, skinless chicken breast, cut into 1-inch pieces
- 10 cups fresh spinach, roughly chopped
- 1 lemon, juiced and zested
- 8 ounces cooked whole-wheat pasta (about half of a 1-pound package)
- ½ cup dry white wine (like Pinot Grigio or Sauvignon Blanc)
- 4 cloves garlic, minced
- ½ cup reduced-fat Parmesan cheese, divided
- 2 tablespoons extra-virgin olive oil
- ½ teaspoon salt
- ¼ teaspoon ground black pepper
- 1 cup full fat cottage cheese

1. Heat olive oil in a large, deep skillet over medium-high heat. Add chicken, salt, and pepper. Cook, stirring occasionally, until just cooked through, about 5-7 minutes.
2. Add minced garlic and cook, stirring, until fragrant, about 1 minute.
3. Stir in white wine, lemon juice, and lemon zest; bring to a simmer. Remove from heat.
4. Stir in spinach, cooked pasta, and cottage cheese. Cover and let stand until the

spinach is just wilted and the cottage cheese is heated through.
5. Divide among 4 plates and top each serving with 2 tablespoons of Parmesan cheese.

Per Serving

Calories: **415** | Carbs: **12g** | Protein: **40g** | Fat: **19g** | Fiber: **3g**

SOUTHWEST TURKEY LASAGNA

Prep time: **20 minutes** | Cook time: **25 minutes** | Serves **8**

- 1 pound lean ground turkey
- 1 medium onion, diced
- 1 green bell pepper, diced
- 1 red bell pepper, diced
- 8 ounces reduced-fat cream cheese, softened
- 1 cup shredded Mexican cheese blend
- ½ cup reduced-fat sour cream
- 6 (8-inch) low-carb whole-wheat tortillas
- 10 ounces enchilada sauce
- ½ cup salsa
- 1 tablespoon chili powder
- Nonstick cooking spray
- 1.5 cups full fat cottage cheese

1. Preheat oven to 400°F. Spray a 13x9-inch baking dish with nonstick cooking spray.
2. In a large skillet over medium heat, cook ground turkey, diced onion, and diced peppers until the turkey is no longer pink. Drain any excess fat.
3. Stir in softened cream cheese and chili powder until well combined.
4. Pour enchilada sauce into a shallow dish. Dip each tortilla in the sauce to coat.
5. Place two tortillas in the prepared baking dish. Spread half of the turkey mixture evenly over the tortillas. Add the cottage cheese over the turkey mixture. Sprinkle 1/3 of the Mexican cheese blend over the cottage cheese. Repeat layers: tortillas, remaining turkey mixture, remaining Mexican cheese. Top with

the last two tortillas and the rest of the cheese.
6. Cover the baking dish with aluminum foil and bake for 20-25 minutes, or until heated through.
7. Let the lasagna rest for 10 minutes before cutting. Serve topped with salsa and sour cream.

Per Serving

Calories: **369** | Carbs: **36g** | Protein: **27g** | Fat: **22g** | Fiber: **19g**

HIGH-PROTEIN COTTAGE CHEESE PIZZA

Prep time: **20 minutes** | Cook time: **1 hour 5 minutes** | Serves **6**

- 8 ounces firm tofu, drained and cut into ½-inch cubes (about 1 ½ cups)
- 1 cup sliced fresh mushrooms
- 2 tablespoons red wine vinegar
- 1 tablespoon olive oil
- 2 teaspoons dried Italian seasoning
- 1 (11-ounce) refrigerated thin pizza crust
- ½ cup pizza sauce
- ½ cup sun-dried tomatoes in oil, drained and chopped
- 1 red bell pepper, thinly sliced
- 1 small onion, thinly sliced
- 1 tablespoon chopped fresh basil leaves
- 1 cup shredded reduced-fat mozzarella cheese (4 ounces)
- 1 cup full fat cottage cheese

1. In a medium bowl, combine tofu, sliced mushrooms, red wine vinegar, olive oil, and Italian seasoning. Cover and refrigerate for at least 30 minutes.
2. Preheat oven to 375°F. Spray a 15x10x1-inch baking pan with nonstick cooking spray. Unroll the pizza crust in the pan. Bake for about 10 minutes, or until the edges are lightly golden brown.
3. Drain the marinade from the tofu and mushrooms, discarding the marinade. Spread pizza sauce over the partially baked crust. Top with tofu, mushrooms, sun-dried tomatoes, sliced red bell pepper, sliced onion, and fresh basil.

4. Bake for 10 minutes. Then, sprinkle shredded mozzarella cheese and dollops of cottage cheese over the pizza. Bake for another 10 minutes, or until the cheese is melted and the crust is deep golden brown.
5. Cut into 6 slices and serve.

Per Serving

Calories: **350** | Fat: **13g** | Carbs: **32g** | Fiber: **3g** | Protein: **13g**

BUFFALO CHICKEN PIZZA

Prep time: **10 minutes** | Cook time: **20 minutes** | Serves **4**

- 1 (10-ounce) ready-to-serve whole-wheat pizza crust
- ¼ cup reduced-fat ranch dressing
- ¼ cup finely chopped celery
- 1 cup cooked chicken breast, cut into bite-sized pieces
- 3 tablespoons Buffalo wing sauce
- ¾ cup green and red bell pepper strips
- ¾ cup shredded reduced-fat mozzarella cheese (31 ounces)
- 1 tablespoon crumbled blue cheese
- 1 cup full fat cottage cheese

1. Preheat oven to 400°F. Place the pizza crust on a large cookie sheet. Spread ranch dressing evenly over the crust. Sprinkle with finely chopped celery.
2. In a small bowl, combine cooked chicken breast and Buffalo wing sauce. Arrange the chicken evenly over the ranch-dressed crust. Top with green and red bell pepper strips.
3. Sprinkle shredded mozzarella cheese and dollops of cottage cheese over the pizza.
4. Bake for 10 minutes, or until the mozzarella cheese is melted and just beginning

to brown. Sprinkle the crumbled blue cheese over the pizza. Bake for an additional 5-10 minutes.
5. Cut into wedges and serve.

Per Serving

Calories: **381** | Fat: **6g** | Carbs: **27g** | Fiber: **3g** | Protein: **16g**

CHAPTER 8: PROTEIN-HEAVY SOUPS AND STEWS

HALIBUT STEW

Prep time: **10 minutes** | Cook time: **15 minutes** | Serves **4**

- 4 slices bacon, chopped
- ½ cup shallots, chopped (or ½ cup yellow onion, chopped)
- 1 teaspoon garlic, minced
- 1 celery stalk, chopped
- 1 parsnip, chopped
- 2 cups fish broth
- 1 tablespoon coconut oil, softened
- 1 pound halibut fillets, cut into 1-inch pieces
- Sea salt and cracked black pepper, to taste
- ¼ teaspoon ground allspice
- 1 cup heavy cream
- 1 cup full-fat cottage cheese, at room temperature

1. Press the "Sauté" button on the Instant Pot. Cook the chopped bacon until crispy.
2. Add chopped shallots (or onion), minced garlic, chopped celery, and chopped parsnip to the Instant Pot. Sauté for 2 minutes, or until the vegetables are slightly tender.
3. Stir in fish broth, softened coconut oil, halibut pieces, salt, black pepper, and ground allspice.
4. Secure the lid. Select "Manual/Pressure Cook" mode on low pressure and cook for 7 minutes. Allow a natural pressure release for 5 minutes, then release the remaining pressure manually.
5. Stir in heavy cream and

cottage cheese. Press the "Sauté" button again and simmer for a few minutes, or until the stew is heated through and the cottage cheese is melted. Serve immediately.

Per Serving

Calories: **532** | Fat: **40g** | Carbs: **10g** | Protein: **35g** | Fiber: **2g**

KETO TACO SOUP

Prep time: **10 minutes** | Cook time: **25 minutes** | Serves **5**

- 2 cups ground beef
- 1 teaspoon onion powder
- 1 tablespoon taco seasoning
- 1 clove garlic, minced
- ½ teaspoon chili flakes
- 1 teaspoon ground cumin
- 1 tablespoon tomato paste
- ½ cup heavy cream
- 5 cups water
- 1 tablespoon coconut oil
- 1 tablespoon cream cheese
- 1 jalapeño pepper, sliced
- 1 cup full fat cottage cheese

1. Press the "Sauté" button on the Instant Pot and melt the coconut oil. Add the ground beef and onion powder. Cook until the beef is browned, breaking it up with a spoon.
2. Add the taco seasoning and minced garlic. Stir well. Sprinkle with chili flakes and ground cumin. Sauté for 10 minutes, stirring every 3 minutes.
3. Add the tomato paste, heavy cream, water, and sliced jalapeño pepper. Stir to combine. Secure the lid and cook on high pressure for 10 minutes.
4. Allow a natural pressure release for 10 minutes, then release any remaining pressure manually.

5. Stir in the cream cheese and cottage cheese until melted.
6. Ladle the soup into bowls and serve.

Per Serving

Calories: **450** | Fat: **35.7g** | Fiber: **3g** | Carbs: **8g** | Protein: **30g**

COCONUT BROCCOLI SOUP

Prep time: **10 minutes** | Cook time: **15 minutes** | Serves **4**

- 1 head broccoli, florets separated
- 4 cups chicken broth
- ¼ teaspoon salt
- 1/8 teaspoon white pepper
- ¼ teaspoon garlic powder
- 1 tablespoon fresh chives, chopped
- 1 cup shredded cheddar cheese
- 1 cup coconut cream
- 1 cup full fat cottage cheese

1. In your Instant Pot, combine the broccoli florets, chicken broth, salt, white pepper, garlic powder, and chives. Stir to combine. Secure the lid and cook on high pressure for 10 minutes.
2. Allow a natural pressure release for 10 minutes, then release any remaining pressure manually.
3. Set the Instant Pot to "Sauté" mode. Add the shredded cheddar cheese, coconut cream, and cottage cheese. Stir until the cheeses are melted and the soup is well combined.
4. Use an immersion blender to blend the soup until smooth and creamy.
5. Cook for 5 more minutes

on "Sauté" mode, stirring occasionally.
6. Ladle the soup into bowls and serve.

Per Serving

Calories: **376** | Fat: **40g** | Carbs: **14g** | Protein: **20g** | Fiber: **4g**

COTTAGE CHEESE ZUCCHINI LEEK SOUP

Prep time: **10 minutes** | Cook time: **17 minutes** | Serves **4**

- 1 tablespoon olive oil
- 1 leek stalk, chopped
- 3 large zucchini, chopped
- 1 medium white onion, chopped
- 2 cloves garlic, minced
- 1 tablespoon mixed dried herbs (Italian seasoning works well)
- 4 cups vegetable broth
- Salt and black pepper, to taste
- 1 cup heavy cream
- 1 cup full-fat cottage cheese

1. Press the "Sauté" button on the Instant Pot and adjust to medium heat.
2. Heat olive oil in the inner pot and sauté the chopped leek, chopped zucchini, and chopped onion until softened, about 5 minutes. Stir in the minced garlic and dried herbs; cook until fragrant, about 30 seconds.
3. Stir in the vegetable broth and season with salt and black pepper.
4. Lock the lid in place; select "Manual/Pressure Cook" mode on high pressure and set the timer for 1 minute.
5. After cooking, allow a natural pressure release for 10 minutes, then release the remaining pressure manually.
6. Use an immersion blender to puree the soup until smooth.

7. Stir in the heavy cream.
8. Dish the soup into serving bowls and top each with a scoop of cottage cheese.
9. Serve warm.

Per Serving

Calories: **319** | Fat: **30g** | Carbs: **12g** | Protein: **18g** | Fiber: **3g**

COTTAGE CHEESE LEEK SOUP

Prep time: **10 minutes** | Cook time: **15 minutes** | Serves **4**

- 7 ounces leeks, chopped (about 2 medium leeks)
- 1 cup shredded Monterey Jack cheese
- 1 teaspoon Italian seasoning
- ½ teaspoon salt
- 4 tablespoons butter
- 2 cups chicken broth
- 1 cup full fat cottage cheese

1. Press the "Sauté" button on the Instant Pot and melt the butter.

2. Add the chopped leeks, salt, and Italian seasoning. Sauté for 5 minutes, stirring occasionally, until the leeks are softened.

3. Add the chicken broth. Secure the lid and cook on high pressure for 10 minutes.

4. Allow a quick pressure release.

5. Add the shredded Monterey Jack cheese and cottage cheese. Stir until the cheeses are melted and the soup is creamy.

6. Serve immediately.

Per Serving

Calories: **358** | Fat: **32g** | Carbs: **8g** | Protein: **20g** | Fiber: **1g**

CHICKEN FAJITA SOUP

Prep time: **10 minutes** | Cook time: **20 minutes** | Serves **4**

- 4 ounces cream cheese
- 12 ounces boneless, skinless chicken breast
- 1 tablespoon taco seasoning
- 2 bell peppers (any color), chopped
- ½ cup canned diced tomatoes
- 3 cups beef broth
- ½ teaspoon salt
- ¼ cup heavy cream
- 1 jalapeño pepper, sliced
- 1 chili pepper (serrano or cayenne), sliced
- 1 tablespoon butter
- ½ teaspoon minced garlic
- 1 cup full fat cottage cheese

1. Press the "Sauté" button on the Instant Pot and melt the butter. Add the chicken breast. Sprinkle with taco seasoning, salt, and minced garlic. Cook for 4 minutes per side, until browned.

2. Add the cream cheese, diced tomatoes, heavy cream, and chopped bell peppers.

3. Secure the lid and cook on high pressure for 10 minutes. Perform a quick pressure release.

4. Remove the chicken and shred it with a fork. Return the shredded chicken to the Instant Pot.

5. Add the sliced chili pepper,

jalapeño pepper, and cottage cheese to the soup. Cook on "Sauté" mode for 5 minutes, stirring until heated through and the cottage cheese is melted.

Per Serving

Calories: **420** | Fat: **33g** | Carbs: **10g** | Protein: **30g** | Fiber: **2g**

FRENCH CARAMELIZED ONION SOUP

Prep time: 10 minutes | Cook time: 15 minutes | Serves 4

- ¼ cup butter, softened
- ¾ pound yellow onions, thinly sliced
- 4 cups beef broth
- ½ teaspoon dried basil
- Kosher salt and ground black pepper, to taste
- ½ cup shredded Swiss cheese
- 1 cup full fat cottage cheese

1. Press the "Sauté" button on the Instant Pot. Once hot, melt the butter and sauté the sliced onions until caramelized and tender.
2. Add beef broth, dried basil, salt, and black pepper.
3. Secure the lid. Select "Manual/Pressure Cook" mode on high pressure and cook for 10 minutes. Perform a quick pressure release.
4. Stir in cottage cheese. Ladle the soup into individual bowls and top with shredded Swiss cheese.

Per Serving

Calories: **328** | Fat: **28g** | Carbs: **18g** | Protein: **22g** | Fiber: **3g**

ROASTED RED PEPPER SOUP

Prep time: 10 minutes | Cook time: 5 minutes | Serves 4

- 2 cups roasted red bell peppers (from a jar or roasted yourself)
- 1 jalapeño pepper, halved and deseeded
- 1 bulb garlic, cloves peeled and crushed
- 6 tomatoes, halved
- 2 cups vegetable broth
- Salt and black pepper, to taste
- 2 tablespoons melted butter
- ½ cup heavy cream
- 3 tablespoons grated Parmesan cheese, for topping
- Roughly chopped chives, for garnish
- 1 cup full fat cottage cheese

1. In the Instant Pot, combine roasted red peppers, jalapeño pepper, crushed garlic cloves, halved tomatoes, vegetable broth, salt, and black pepper.
2. Secure the lid. Select "Manual/Pressure Cook" mode on high pressure and set the timer for 5 minutes. Perform a quick pressure release.
3. Use an immersion blender to puree the ingredients until smooth.
4. Stir in melted butter, heavy cream, and cottage cheese until melted. Adjust seasoning with salt and black pepper.
5. Ladle the soup into bowls and top with grated Parmesan cheese and chopped chives. Serve warm.

Per Serving

Calories: **332** | Fat: **28g** | Carbs: **15g** | Protein: **18g** | Fiber: **4g**

HERBY CHEESE SOUP

Prep time: **10 minutes** | Cook time: **8 minutes** | Serves **4**

- 1 tablespoon olive oil
- 4 tablespoons butter
- 1 small white onion, roughly chopped
- 3 cloves garlic, minced
- ¼ cup mixed fresh herbs (parsley, thyme, rosemary)
- 2 cups peeled and cubed turnips
- 3 cups vegetable broth
- Salt and black pepper, to taste
- 1 cup almond milk
- 1 cup shredded cheddar cheese
- 2 tablespoons chopped scallions, for garnish
- 1 cup full fat cottage cheese

1. Press the "Sauté" button on the Instant Pot and adjust to medium heat.
2. Heat butter and olive oil in the Instant Pot. Add chopped onion and minced garlic. Cook until softened, about 3 minutes.
3. Add turnips, vegetable broth, salt, black pepper, and fresh herbs.
4. Secure the lid. Select "Manual/Pressure Cook" mode on high pressure and set the timer for 5 minutes. Perform a quick pressure release.
5. Add shredded cheddar cheese, almond milk, and cottage cheese. Use an immersion blender to puree

the soup until smooth. Adjust seasoning with salt and black pepper.
6. Ladle the soup into bowls and top with chopped scallions. Serve warm.

Per Serving

Calories:**431** | Fat: **35g** | Carbs: **16g** | Protein: **20g** | Fiber: **3g**

BROCCOLI CHEESE SOUP

Prep time: **10 minutes** | Cook time: **5 minutes** | Serves **4**

- 2 cups broccoli florets
- 1 cup shredded cheddar cheese
- 2 cloves garlic, minced
- 1 tablespoon olive oil
- 1 cup heavy cream
- 2 cups chicken broth
- ½ teaspoon ground black pepper
- 1 cup full fat cottage cheese

1. Press the "Sauté" button on the Instant Pot and heat olive oil.
2. Add minced garlic and sauté for 2 minutes.
3. Add broccoli florets, shredded cheddar cheese, heavy cream, chicken broth, and black pepper.
4. Secure the lid. Select "Manual/Pressure Cook" mode on high pressure and cook for 3 minutes.
5. Allow a natural pressure release for 5 minutes, then release any remaining pressure manually.
6. Stir in the cottage cheese.

7. Serve immediately.

Per Serving

Calories: **385** | Fat: **34g** | Carbs: **10g** | Protein: **20g** | Fiber: **2g**

CHAPTER 9: PROTEIN-RICH SNACKS

EGG BITES

Prep time: **5 minutes** | Cook time: **30 minutes** | Serves **6**

- 5 large eggs
- 1 cup Swiss cheese, shredded
- 1 cup full-fat cottage cheese
- ⅛ teaspoon salt
- ⅛ teaspoon black pepper
- 2 strips no-sugar-added bacon, cooked and crumbled
- 1 tablespoon fresh chives, finely chopped (optional)
- Cooking spray or cupcake liners

1. Preheat oven to 350°F.

2. Grease a 6-cup muffin tin with cooking spray or line with cupcake liners.

3. In a large bowl, whisk the eggs until well beaten.

4. Add the shredded Swiss cheese, cottage cheese, salt, and pepper to the beaten eggs. Whisk until thoroughly combined.

5. Pour the egg mixture evenly into the prepared muffin cups, filling each about ¾ full.

6. Sprinkle the crumbled bacon evenly over the top of each egg bite.

7. Bake for 25-30 minutes until the egg bites are set and a toothpick inserted in the

center comes out clean.

7. Allow to cool in the pan for 5 minutes, then carefully remove and serve warm, garnished with chopped chives if desired.

Per Serving

Calories: **182** | Fat: **11g** | Protein: **16g** | Fiber: **0g** | Carbs: **3g**

CAULIFLOWER TOTS

Prep time: **10 minutes** | Cook time: **16 minutes** | Serves **4**

- 1 medium cauliflower head, cut into florets
- 1½ cups water
- ½ cup sharp cheddar cheese, shredded
- 4 egg whites
- 2 tablespoons unsalted butter
- 2 tablespoons heavy cream
- ½ cup 2% milkfat cottage cheese
- ½ teaspoon garlic powder
- Salt and black pepper to taste
- ¼ teaspoon paprika (optional)

1. Pour the water into your Instant Pot. Place the cauliflower florets inside the steamer basket and lower

the basket into the pot. Seal the lid and cook on High pressure for 3 minutes.

2. After the beep, perform a quick pressure release. Transfer the cauliflower florets to a large bowl and allow to cool. Discard the water and wipe the pot clean.

3. When the cauliflower is cool enough to handle, add the shredded cheddar, egg whites, heavy cream, cottage cheese, garlic powder, salt, pepper, and paprika (if using) to the bowl with the cauliflower.

4. Using a potato masher or fork, mash the mixture until well combined but still slightly chunky for texture.

5. Wet your hands to prevent sticking and form the mixture into small tot-shaped nuggets (about 1½

inches long).

6. Set the Instant Pot to Sauté mode and melt the butter. Working in batches, cook the cauliflower tots until golden brown on both sides, about 2-3 minutes per side.

7. Transfer to a paper towel-lined plate to absorb excess butter before serving.

Per Serving

Calories: **255** | Fat: **16g** | Carbs: **8g** | Protein: **14g** | Fiber: **3g**

DOUBLE CHEESE BITES

Prep time: **5 minutes** | Cook time: **15 minutes** |Makes **12 Bites**

- 10 ounces Swiss cheese, shredded
- 10 ounces 4% milkfat cottage cheese
- ¼ cup sour cream
- 1 tablespoon dill pickle, finely minced
- ½ teaspoon sea salt
- ¼ teaspoon freshly ground black pepper
- 1 teaspoon granulated garlic
- ¾ cup pecans, finely chopped
- 1 tablespoon fresh chives, minced (optional for garnish)

1. In a large mixing bowl, combine the shredded Swiss cheese, cottage cheese, sour cream, minced pickle, salt, pepper, and granulated garlic. Beat with an electric mixer on medium speed until everything is well incorporated and smooth, about 2 minutes.
2. Cover the mixture and refrigerate for at least 2 hours or overnight to firm up.
3. Using a tablespoon or small cookie scoop, portion the chilled mixture and form into bite-sized balls with your hands. If the mixture becomes too sticky, refrigerate for 30 minutes before continuing.
4. Place the chopped pecans

in a shallow dish. Roll each cheese ball in the chopped pecans, pressing gently to coat them evenly.
5. Arrange on a serving platter, sprinkle with minced chives if using, and serve chilled.

Per Serving (2 bites)

Calories: 398 | Fat: 31g | Carbs: 9.4g | Protein: 22.6g | Fiber: 1.8g

THREE-CHEESE AND BEER DIP

Prep time: **10 minutes** | Cook time: **10 minutes** | Serves **10**

- 16 ounces full-fat cottage cheese, at room temperature
- 5 ounces goat cheese, softened
- ½ teaspoon garlic powder
- 1 teaspoon stone-ground mustard
- ½ cup chicken stock, preferably homemade
- ½ cup lager beer
- 6 ounces pancetta, finely chopped
- 1 cup Monterey Jack cheese, shredded
- 2 tablespoons fresh chives, roughly chopped
- Assorted crackers, pretzels, or vegetables for serving

1. Add cottage cheese, goat cheese, garlic powder, mustard, chicken stock, beer, and pancetta to the Instant Pot.
2. Secure the lid and set the valve to sealing position. Select "Manual" or "Pressure Cook" mode and set to High pressure; cook for 4 minutes.
3. Once cooking is complete, perform a quick pressure release by carefully turning the valve to venting. When the float valve drops, carefully remove the lid.
4. Press the "Sauté" button to heat up your Instant Pot. Add the shredded Monterey Jack cheese and stir continuously until the cheese is fully melted and

the dip is smooth and well combined, about 2-3 minutes.
5. Transfer to a serving bowl, sprinkle with fresh chopped chives, and serve warm with your choice of dippers.

Per Serving

Calories: 280 | Fat: 20g | Carbs: 6g | Protein: 16g | Fiber: 0g

GRILLED BALSAMIC MELON AND CHEESE

Prep time: **5 minutes** | Cook time: **10 minutes** | Serves **4**

- 4 cups cantaloupe or honeydew melon, cut into 1-inch cubes
- 2 tablespoons balsamic glaze
- 2 tablespoons extra virgin olive oil
- 1 teaspoon dried oregano
- ½ teaspoon salt
- ½ teaspoon freshly ground black pepper
- 1 cup 2% cottage cheese
- ½ cup crumbled feta cheese
- 4 tablespoons chopped fresh basil

1. Preheat a grill or grill pan over medium heat.
2. In a bowl, toss the melon cubes with balsamic glaze, olive oil, oregano, salt, and pepper.
3. Thread the melon cubes onto skewers and grill for 5 minutes per side until slightly caramelized.
4. Remove from the grill and place on a serving plate. Top with cottage cheese, crumbled feta, and fresh basil.

5. Drizzle with additional balsamic glaze if desired and serve immediately.

Per Serving

Calorie: **350** | Fat: **22g** | Carbs: **22g** | Protein: **18g** | Fiber: **2g**

SPANISH COTTAGE CHEESE BOMBS

Prep time: **10 minutes** | Cook time: **10 minutes** | Serves **8**

- 1 tablespoon beef tallow, melted
- 1 medium yellow onion, chopped
- 1 pound chorizo sausage
- 1 garlic clove, minced
- 1 red bell pepper, chopped
- 1 cup chicken broth
- ½ teaspoon deli mustard
- 1 plum tomato, puréed
- 1 cup cottage cheese, drained
- ⅓ cup mayonnaise
- 4 ounces cream cheese, softened

1. Press the "Sauté" button on your Instant Pot and melt the tallow. Once hot, cook the onion until tender and translucent, about 3-4 minutes.
2. Add chorizo and garlic to your Instant Pot; cook until the sausage is no longer pink, crumbling the sausage with a fork as it cooks.
3. Stir in bell pepper, broth, mustard, and tomato.
4. Secure the lid. Select "Manual" mode and High pressure; cook for 4 minutes. Once cooking is complete, use a quick pressure release; carefully remove the lid.
5. Allow mixture to cool slightly, then add the cottage cheese, cream cheese, and mayo. Stir until

well combined.
6. Shape the mixture into 2-inch balls and refrigerate for 30 minutes to firm up before serving.

Per Serving

Calories: **427** | Fat: **36g** | Carbs: **8g** | Protein: **18g** | Fiber: **1g**

ROASTED PEPPER AND COTTAGE CHEESE DIP

Prep time: **10 minutes** | Cook time: **10 minutes** | Serves **6**

- 1 cup heavy cream
- 2 (12 oz) jars roasted red bell peppers, drained and finely chopped
- 2 garlic cloves, minced
- 2 cups cottage cheese, pureed in blender until smooth
- 1 teaspoon red pepper flakes
- 8 oz cream cheese, softened
- 2 tablespoons fresh chives, chopped (optional)

1. Combine the heavy cream and roasted peppers in the inner pot of your Instant Pot.
2. Lock the lid in place; select Manual mode on High Pressure and set the timer to 3 minutes.
3. After cooking, perform a quick pressure release to let out all the steam, and open the lid.
4. Set the Instant Pot to Sauté mode and mix in the cottage cheese, cream cheese, garlic, and red pepper flakes. Stir until the cream cheese melts, about 3 minutes.
5. Turn off the heat and let the dip cool slightly.
6. Spoon the dip into serving

bowls, garnish with chives if desired, and serve with vegetable sticks or pork rinds.

Per Serving

Calories: **392** | Fat: **24g** | Carbs: **6g** | Protein: **10g** | Fiber: **1g**

PARMESAN COTTAGE CHEESE CHICKEN WINGS

Prep time: **10 minutes** | Cook time: **20 minutes** | Serves **12**

- 4 pounds chicken wings, cut into sections
- ½ cup butter, melted
- 1 tablespoon Italian seasoning mix
- ½ teaspoon onion powder
- ½ teaspoon garlic powder
- 1 teaspoon paprika
- ½ teaspoon coarse sea salt
- ½ teaspoon ground black pepper
- 1 cup cottage cheese, drained
- ½ cup Parmesan cheese, grated
- 2 eggs, lightly whisked

1. Add chicken wings, butter, Italian seasoning mix, onion powder, garlic powder, paprika, salt, and black pepper to your Instant Pot.
2. Secure the lid. Choose "Poultry" mode and High pressure. Cook the chicken wings for 10 minutes. Once cooking is complete, use a natural pressure release; carefully remove the lid.
3. In a bowl, mix cottage cheese, Parmesan cheese, and eggs. Spoon this mixture over the wings.
4. Secure the lid. Choose "Manual" mode and High pressure; cook for 4 minutes longer. Once cooking is complete, use a quick pressure release; carefully remove the lid.

5. For extra crispiness, place wings on a baking sheet and broil for 2-3 minutes.
6. Serve hot and enjoy!

Per Serving

Calories: **443** | Fat: **25g** | Carbs: **3g** | Protein: **28g** | Fiber: **0g**

COTTAGE CHEESE AND OLIVE SCONES

Prep time: **10 minutes** | Cook time: **30 minutes** | Serves **4**

- 3 cups almond flour, sifted
- 2 tablespoons baking powder
- ¼ teaspoon salt
- ⅛ teaspoon cayenne pepper
- 2 tablespoons butter, cold and cubed
- 1 cup cottage cheese, well-drained
- ½ cup shredded cheddar cheese
- ¼ cup Kalamata olives, pitted and chopped
- 1 cup unsweetened almond milk

1. In a medium bowl, mix the almond flour, baking powder, salt, and cayenne pepper. Cut in the butter until crumbs form.
2. Fold in the drained cottage cheese, cheddar cheese, and olives.
3. Gradually add almond milk, stirring until the dough is soft enough to handle.
4. Turn the dough onto a clean work surface dusted with almond flour and gently knead into a 1-inch thick round.
5. Cut the dough into 4 wedges and shape into 3-inch scones.
6. Pour 1 ½ cups of water into the inner pot of your Instant Pot, place the trivet inside, and arrange the scones on top (you may need to cook in batches).
7. Lock the lid in place; select Manual mode on High Pressure, and set the timer for 20 minutes.

8. Once done baking, allow for a natural pressure release for 10 minutes, then perform a quick release for any remaining pressure before opening the lid.
9. Transfer the scones to a wire rack to cool slightly before serving.

Per Serving

Calories: **510** | Fat: **40g** | Carbs: **20g** | Protein: **22g** | Fiber: **8g**

SPICY SAUSAGE AND COTTAGE CHEESE DIP

Prep time: **10 minutes** | Cook time: **25 minutes** | Serves **6**

- 12 oz Italian sausages, casings removed
- 1 jalapeño pepper, seeded and chopped
- 1 cup cottage cheese, drained
- 5 oz cheddar cheese, shredded
- 1 teaspoon coconut oil
- 1 tablespoon tomato paste
- ¼ cup heavy cream
- 1 teaspoon Italian seasoning
- ¼ teaspoon garlic powder

1. Select "Sauté" mode on your Instant Pot and heat the coconut oil.
2. Add Italian sausages and cook for 10 minutes, breaking up the meat with a wooden spoon every 3 minutes.
3. Add jalapeño pepper, tomato paste, Italian seasoning, and garlic powder. Sauté for 2 more minutes.
4. Stir in the heavy cream.
5. Close the lid and set to "Manual" mode (high pressure) for 10 minutes.
6. When cooking is complete, perform a quick pressure release.
7. Open the lid and stir in the drained cottage cheese and shredded cheddar until well combined and melted.

8. Transfer to a serving bowl and serve hot with celery sticks, bell pepper slices, or pork rinds.

Per Serving

Calories: **371** | Fat: **24.2g** | Fiber: **0.1g** | Carbs: **0.9g** | Protein: **12.1g**

CHAPTER 10: PROTEIN-ENHANCED DESSERTS

COTTAGE CHEESE STRAWBERRY CREPES

Prep time: 10 minutes | Cook time: 10 minutes | Serves 4

- ½ cup old-fashioned rolled oats
- 1 cup unsweetened plain almond milk
- 1 large egg
- 3 teaspoons honey, divided
- Nonstick cooking spray
- 2 ounces reduced-fat cream cheese, softened
- ¼ cup low-fat cottage cheese
- 2 cups sliced fresh strawberries

1. In a blender, process the rolled oats until they resemble flour. Add the almond milk, egg, and 1 ½ teaspoons honey, and blend until smooth.
2. Heat a large nonstick skillet or crepe pan over medium heat. Spray with nonstick cooking spray.
3. Pour ¼ cup of the oat batter onto the hot skillet and quickly swirl to coat the bottom of the pan. Cook for 2 to 3 minutes, or until the edges begin to brown. Flip the crepe with a spatula and cook for about 1 minute, until lightly browned and firm. Transfer to a plate. Repeat with the remaining batter, spraying the skillet with nonstick cooking spray before each crepe. Cover the cooked crepes loosely with aluminum foil to keep warm.
4. Clean the blender. Add the softened cream cheese, cottage cheese, and the remaining 1 ½ teaspoons

honey. Blend until smooth.
5. Spread each crepe with 2 tablespoons of the cream cheese mixture. Top with ¼ cup of sliced strawberries. Fold or roll the crepes and serve.

Per Serving

Calories: **149** | Fat: **6g** | Protein: **6g** | Carbs: **20g** | Fiber: **3g**

PEACH COBBLER

Prep time: 10 minutes | Cook time: 30 minutes | Serves 6

- 3 tablespoons fruit preserves (blueberry, raspberry, strawberry, or mixed-fruit)
- 1 (15-ounce) can diced peaches in water or 100% juice, drained
- ½ cup 2% cottage cheese
- ½ cup water
- 2 scoops vanilla protein powder
- ¼ cup all-purpose flour
- ⅓ cup granulated sugar substitute (like Truvia or Splenda)
- ½ cup quick-cooking rolled oats
- 1 tablespoon honey

1. Preheat oven to 350°F. Spray an 8-inch square baking dish with nonstick cooking spray.
2. Spread the fruit preserves evenly in the bottom of the baking dish. Top with the drained diced peaches.
3. In a medium bowl, combine cottage cheese, water, vanilla protein powder, all-purpose flour, and sugar substitute. Mix well and pour over the peaches.
4. In a small bowl, mix the quick-cooking rolled oats and honey. Spoon the oat mixture over the top of the cobbler.
5. Bake for about 30 minutes, or until golden brown. Let

the cobbler cool for at least 20 minutes before serving.

Per Serving

- Calorie: 261 | Fat: 5g | Carbs: 35g | Protein: 15g | Fiber: 3g

MANGO COCONUT COTTAGE CHEESE MOUSSE

Prep time: 15 minutes | Cook time: 5 minutes | Serves 2

- 10 ounces full-fat cottage cheese
- ½ cup frozen mango chunks
- ¼ cup full-fat coconut milk (from a can, not the carton)
- 2 tablespoons shredded unsweetened coconut, plus more for topping
- 1 tablespoon lime juice
- 1 tablespoon maple syrup (or honey)
- Pinch of ground ginger (optional)
- Fresh mint leaves, for garnish

1. Combine the cottage cheese, frozen mango chunks, coconut milk, shredded coconut, lime juice, maple syrup (or honey), and ground ginger (if using) in a blender.
2. Blend until completely smooth and creamy. You might need to stop and scrape down the sides a couple of times to ensure everything is incorporated.
3. Pour the mousse mixture into two serving glasses or bowls.
4. Sprinkle the top of each serving with extra shredded coconut and garnish with a few fresh mint leaves.

5. Chill in the refrigerator for at least 20 minutes to allow the mousse to firm up slightly.

Per Serving

Calories: **280** | Fat: **18g** | Carbs: **20g** | Protein: **20g** | Fiber: **4g**

POBLANO AND CHEESE FRITTATA

Prep time: 10 minutes | Cook time: 50 minutes | Serves 4

- Vegetable oil or butter, for greasing the pan
- 4 large eggs
- 1 cup half-and-half
- 1 (10-ounce) can chopped green chilies, drained
- 1 ½ teaspoons salt
- ½ teaspoon ground cumin
- 1 cup Mexican blend shredded cheese, divided
- ¼ cup chopped fresh cilantro
- 1 cup full fat cottage cheese

1. Grease a 6-by-3-inch pan well with oil or butter.
2. In a medium bowl, beat the eggs and stir in the half-and-half, drained green chilies, salt, ground cumin,

and ½ cup of the shredded Mexican cheese. Add the cottage cheese and stir to combine. Pour the mixture into the prepared pan and cover with aluminum foil.
3. Pour 2 cups of water into the Instant Pot and place the trivet inside. Place the pan on the trivet.
4. Secure the lid. Select "Manual/Pressure Cook" mode on high pressure and cook for 20 minutes. Allow a natural pressure release for 10 minutes, then release any remaining pressure manually. Remove the pan from the Instant Pot and remove the foil.
5. Scatter the remaining ½ cup of shredded Mexican cheese on top of the frittata. Place it under a hot broiler for 2-5 minutes, or until the cheese

is bubbling and browned.
6. Let the frittata sit for 5-10 minutes. Gently loosen the sides from the pan with a knife. Invert the frittata onto a plate. If desired, flip it onto a plate once more to have the cheese side up.

Per Serving

Calories: **283** | Fat: **22g** | Carbs: **7g** | Fiber: **1g** | Protein: **16g**

PEANUT CHEESECAKE

Prep time: **10 minutes** | Cook time: **8 hours** | Serves **4**

- 1 cup cream cheese, softened
- 4 large eggs, beaten
- 1 teaspoon vanilla extract
- ¼ cup coconut milk
- 1 teaspoon coconut oil, melted
- 1 tablespoon erythritol (or another sugar substitute)
- 2 ounces chopped peanuts
- 1 cup water
- 1 cup full fat cottage cheese

1. Mix together the softened cream cheese, beaten eggs, vanilla extract, coconut milk, melted coconut oil, erythritol, chopped peanuts, and cottage cheese in a bowl until smooth.
2. Pour the mixture into an Instant Pot-safe baking pan. Flatten the surface if desired.
3. Pour 1 cup of water into the Instant Pot and place the baking pan on the trivet inside.
4. Close the lid and cook on "Low" mode (or "Slow Cook") for 8 hours.

5. Allow to cool before serving.

Per Serving

Calories: **393** | Fat: **6.3g** | Fiber: **1.5g** | Carbs: **8.9g** | Protein: **13.9g**

FLUFFY BERRY CUPCAKES

Prep time: **10 minutes** | Cook time: **30 minutes** | Serves **6**

- ¼ cup coconut oil, softened
- 3 ounces cream cheese, softened
- ¼ cup heavy cream
- 4 large eggs
- ¼ cup coconut flour
- ¼ cup almond flour
- Pinch of salt
- ⅓ cup granulated sugar substitute (like Swerve)
- 1 teaspoon baking powder
- ¼ teaspoon ground cardamom
- ½ teaspoon ground star anise
- ½ cup fresh mixed berries
- 1 cup full fat cottage cheese

1. Pour 1 ½ cups of water into the Instant Pot and place a metal rack inside.

2. In a large bowl, mix the softened coconut oil, softened cream cheese, and heavy cream. Fold in the eggs, one at a time, mixing until well combined.
3. In a separate bowl, thoroughly combine the coconut flour, almond flour, salt, granulated sugar substitute, baking powder, ground cardamom, and ground star anise.
4. Add the cream/egg mixture to the dry flour mixture. Then, fold in the fresh mixed berries and cottage cheese, gently stirring to combine.
5. Divide the batter evenly among silicone cupcake liners. Cover each liner with a piece of aluminum foil. Place the cupcakes on the rack in the Instant Pot.
6. Secure the lid. Select "Manual/Pressure Cook"

mode on high pressure and cook for 25 minutes. Allow a natural pressure release for 10 minutes, then release any remaining pressure manually. Carefully remove the cupcakes from the Instant Pot and let them cool before serving.

Per Serving

Calories: **382** | Fat: **30g** | Carbs: **12g** | Protein: **15g** | Fiber: **3g**

CHOCOLATE PROTEIN CREPES

Prep time: 5 minutes | Cook time: 40 minutes | Makes 10 crepes

- 1 medium banana
- 2 scoops chocolate vegan protein powder
- 2 ¼ cups unsweetened vanilla almond milk
- 1 large egg
- 6 tablespoons egg whites
- 1 teaspoon vanilla extract
- 1 ½ cups oat flour
- Pinch of sea salt
- 1 tablespoon coconut oil
- Sugar-free chocolate sauce (optional)
- Sliced strawberries (optional)
- Crushed peanuts (optional)
- 1 cup reduced-fat cottage cheese (optional)

1. In a high-speed blender, combine the banana, protein powder, almond milk, egg, egg whites, vanilla extract, oat flour, and sea salt. Blend until smooth.
2. Heat enough coconut oil to coat a large griddle or skillet over medium heat. Pour or scoop about ¼ cup of the crepe batter onto the hot griddle at a time. Cook for about 2 minutes, or until lightly browned on one side. Flip and cook for 2 minutes on the other side, until lightly browned. Repeat with the remaining batter and coconut oil.
3. Serve the crepes topped with sugar-free chocolate sauce, sliced strawberries, crushed peanuts, and/or a dollop of cottage cheese.

Per Serving

Calories: **229** | Fat: **8g** | Protein: **12g** | Carbs: **28g** | Fiber: **5g**

PEANUT BUTTER CHEESECAKE BITES

Prep time: 10 minutes | Cook time: 15 minutes | Serves 8

- 16 ounces (454g) cream cheese, softened
- 1 cup powdered erythritol (or another sugar substitute)
- ½ cup peanut flour
- ¼ cup sour cream
- 2 teaspoons vanilla extract
- 2 large eggs
- 2 cups water
- ¼ cup sugar-free chocolate chips
- 1 tablespoon coconut oil
- 1 cup full fat cottage cheese

1. In a large bowl, beat the softened cream cheese and powdered erythritol until smooth. Gently fold in the peanut flour, sour cream, vanilla extract, and cottage cheese. Fold in the eggs slowly until just combined.
2. Pour the batter evenly into four 4-inch springform pans or silicone cupcake molds. Cover each with aluminum foil. Pour 2 cups of water into the Instant Pot and place the trivet inside.
3. Carefully lower the pans into the Instant Pot. Select "Manual/Pressure Cook" mode on high pressure and set the timer for 15 minutes. Allow a full natural pressure release. Carefully remove the pans from the Instant Pot and let them cool completely before refrigerating.
4. In a small bowl, microwave the sugar-free chocolate

chips and coconut oil for 30 seconds and whisk until smooth. Drizzle the chocolate over the cheesecakes. Chill in the refrigerator before serving.

Per Serving

Calories: **263** | Fat: **23g** | Protein: **7g** | Carbs: **7g** | Fiber: **1g**

CHERRY MINI CAKES

Prep time: **10 minutes** | **Cook time: 25 minutes** | Serves **6**

- 4 large eggs, beaten
- ⅓ cup granulated sugar substitute (like Swerve)
- 2 tablespoons coconut oil, melted
- 4 ounces cream cheese, softened
- ½ cup plain Greek yogurt
- 1 teaspoon vanilla extract
- ½ cup almond flour
- ½ cup coconut flour
- ¼ teaspoon grated nutmeg
- ¼ teaspoon salt
- 1 teaspoon baking powder
- ½ teaspoon baking soda
- ½ cup pitted cherries, halved
- 1 cup full fat cottage cheese

1. Pour 1 ½ cups of water into the Instant Pot and place a metal rack inside. Spray 6 ramekins with nonstick cooking spray.
2. In a large bowl, whisk together the beaten eggs and sugar substitute until smooth. Add the melted coconut oil, softened cream cheese, Greek yogurt, and vanilla extract. Mix until well combined.
3. In a separate bowl, whisk together the almond flour, coconut flour, grated nutmeg, salt, baking powder, and baking soda. Add this dry mixture to the egg mixture and stir until just combined.
4. Fold in the halved pitted cherries and cottage cheese, gently stirring to combine. Pour the batter evenly into the prepared ramekins.
5. Place the ramekins on the metal rack in the Instant Pot. Secure the lid. Select "Manual/Pressure Cook" mode on high pressure and cook for 20 minutes. Allow

a natural pressure release for 10 minutes, then release any remaining pressure manually.
6. Carefully remove the ramekins from the Instant Pot and transfer them to a cooling rack. Loosen the sides of the cakes from the ramekins and invert them onto plates. Serve chilled.

Per Serving

Calories: 255 | **Fat: 20g** | **Carbs: 12g** | **Protein: 15g** | **Fiber: 3g**

LEMON CHEESECAKE

Prep time: **10 minutes** | **Cook time: 40 minutes** | Serves **6**

- ⅓ cup whole-milk cottage cheese
- 2 large eggs
- 2 cups water
- 1 (8-ounce) package cream cheese, softened
- ¼ cup powdered erythritol (or another sugar substitute)
- Juice and zest of 1 lemon
- ½ teaspoon lemon extract

1. Combine the cottage cheese, cream cheese, powdered erythritol, lemon juice, lemon zest, and lemon extract in a mixing bowl.
2. Beat until the mixture is smooth. Adjust erythritol to taste.
3. Lower the mixer speed and blend in the eggs until fully incorporated, being careful not to overmix.
4. Grease a 6-inch springform pan and pour in the cheesecake mixture.
5. Cover the pan tightly with aluminum foil and place it on the trivet inside the Instant Pot.
6. Pour 2 cups of water into the Instant Pot, then close and lock the lid.
7. Press the "Manual/Pressure Cook" button and set the timer for 30 minutes on high pressure.
8. When the timer goes off, allow a natural pressure release for 10 minutes,

then release any remaining pressure manually.
9. Carefully remove the cheesecake from the Instant Pot and let it cool slightly.
10. Chill the cheesecake in the refrigerator for at least 8 hours before serving.

Per Serving

Calories: 220 | **Fat: 22g** | **Carbs: 5g** | **Protein: 10g** | **Fiber: 0g**

MEASUREMENT CONVERSION CHART

VOLUME EQUIVALENTS(DRY)

US STANDARD	METRIC (APPROXIMATE)
1/8 teaspoon	0.5 mL
1/4 teaspoon	1 mL
1/2 teaspoon	2 mL
3/4 teaspoon	4 mL
1 teaspoon	5 mL
1 tablespoon	15 mL
1/4 cup	59 mL
1/2 cup	118 mL
3/4 cup	177 mL
1 cup	235 mL
2 cups	475 mL
3 cups	700 mL
4 cups	1 L

WEIGHT EQUIVALENTS

US STANDARD	METRIC (APPROXIMATE)
1 ounce	28 g
2 ounces	57 g
5 ounces	142 g
10 ounces	284 g
15 ounces	425 g
16 ounces (1 pound)	455 g
1.5 pounds	680 g
2 pounds	907 g

VOLUME EQUIVALENTS(LIQUID)

US STANDARD	US STANDARD (OUNCES)	METRIC (APPROXIMATE)
2 tablespoons	1 fl.oz.	30 mL
1/4 cup	2 fl.oz.	60 mL
1/2 cup	4 fl.oz.	120 mL
1 cup	8 fl.oz.	240 mL
1 1/2 cup	12 fl.oz.	355 mL
2 cups or 1 pint	16 fl.oz.	475 mL
4 cups or 1 quart	32 fl.oz.	1 L
1 gallon	128 fl.oz.	4 L

TEMPERATURES EQUIVALENTS

FAHRENHEIT(F)	CELSIUS(C) (APPROXIMATE)
225 °F	107 °C
250 °F	120 °C
275 °F	135 °C
300 °F	150 °C
325 °F	160 °C
350 °F	180 °C
375 °F	190 °C
400 °F	205 °C
425 °F	220 °C
450 °F	235 °C
475 °F	245 °C
500 °F	260 °C

The Dirty Dozen and Clean Fifteen

The Environmental Working Group (EWG) is a nonprofit, nonpartisan organization dedicated to protecting human health and the environment Its mission is to empower people to live healthier lives in a healthier environment. This organization publishes an annual list of the twelve kinds of produce, in sequence, that have the highest amount of pesticide residue-the Dirty Dozen-as well as a list of the fifteen kinds ofproduce that have the least amount of pesticide residue-the Clean Fifteen.

THE DIRTY DOZEN	THE CLEAN FIFTEEN
• The 2016 Dirty Dozen includes the following produce. These are considered among the year's most important produce to buy organic:	• The least critical to buy organically are the Clean Fifteen list. The following are on the 2016 list:

THE DIRTY DOZEN

Strawberries	Spinach
Apples	Tomatoes
Nectarines	Bell peppers
Peaches	Cherry tomatoes
Celery	Cucumbers
Grapes	Kale/collard greens
Cherries	Hot peppers

• *The Dirty Dozen list contains two additional itemskale/collard greens and hot peppers-because they tend to contain trace levels of highly hazardous pesticides.*

THE CLEAN FIFTEEN

Avocados	Papayas
Corn	Kiw
Pineapples	Eggplant
Cabbage	Honeydew
Sweet peas	Grapefruit
Onions	Cantaloupe
Asparagus	Cauliflower
Mangos	

• *Some of the sweet corn sold in the United States are made from genetically engineered (GE) seedstock. Buy organic varieties of these crops to avoid GE produce.*

APPENDIX 3: INDEX

A

apple........................ 19, 27, 29

avocado......................... 25, 26

B

banana 13, 19, 20, 21, 59

beef chuck 31

beef tallow...........................52

breadcrumbs.......................33

broccoli.................... 32, 45, 48

C

cauliflower 31, 34, 50

chicken breast.............. 25, 28,
    29, 40, 41, 42, 46

chicken broth 31, 39,
    40, 45, 46, 48, 52

chicken wings.......................53

coconut water 18, 19, 23

cucumber..................... 19, 25,
    26, 27

E

eggs 12, 13, 14,
    15, 16, 29, 35, 50, 53, 57,
    58, 59, 60

H

ham.............................. 14, 31

heavy cream 26, 28,
    35, 44, 45, 46, 47, 48, 50,
    53, 54, 58

J

jalapeño pepper 44, 46,
    47, 54

K

kale 19, 39

L

leeks 46

M

macaroni..............................33

mango 20, 23, 33, 57

maple syrup................. 13, 16,
    19, 20, 22, 33, 57

mayonnaise............ 14, 25, 26,
    27, 29, 52

N

nutmeg....................22, 33, 60

O

oats.............. 13, 16, 21, 22, 56

oregano..............15, 25, 34, 52

P

paprika 26, 27, 39, 50, 53

pork 27, 35, 53, 54

pork chops...........................27

Q

quinoa 25

R

raspberries 16, 21, 22, 23

rosemary..... 15, 31, 34, 36, 48

S

shrimp.................................27

strawberries 19, 21,
    22, 23, 56, 59

T

turkey thighs 31

V

vanilla extract.............. 12, 19,
    20, 21, 22, 58, 59, 60

vegetable broth..................45,
    47, 48

Y

yogurt 13, 15,
    16, 18, 21, 22, 23, 60

Z

zucchini 15, 34, 45